AEGYPTIACA

15. DICTAEAN CAVE. SCALE $\frac{1}{1}$

AEGYPTIACA

A CATALOGUE

OF

EGYPTIAN OBJECTS IN THE AEGEAN AREA

BY

J. D. S. PENDLEBURY

BEATSON SCHOLAR OF PEMBROKE COLLEGE, CAMBRIDGE
UNIVERSITY STUDENT OF THE BRITISH SCHOOL OF
ARCHAEOLOGY IN ATHENS 1927–28, MEMBER
OF EGYPT EXPLORATION SOCIETY'S
EXPEDITION 1928–29

WITH A FOREWORD BY

H. R. HALL

KEEPER OF EGYPTIAN AND ASSYRIAN ANTIQUITIES
IN THE BRITISH MUSEUM

CAMBRIDGE
AT THE UNIVERSITY PRESS
mcmxxx

CAMBRIDGE
UNIVERSITY PRESS

University Printing House, Cambridge CB2 8BS, United Kingdom

Published in the United States of America by Cambridge University Press, New York

Cambridge University Press is part of the University of Cambridge.

It furthers the University's mission by disseminating knowledge in the pursuit of education, learning and research at the highest international levels of excellence.

www.cambridge.org
Information on this title: www.cambridge.org/9781107418905

© Cambridge University Press 1930

First published 1930
First paperback edition 2014

A catalogue record for this publication is available from the British Library

ISBN 978-1-107-41890-5 Paperback

To

MY FATHER

PREFACE

THIS small book, outcome of two years' studentship in Greece and a season's excavation in Egypt, is an attempt—the first so far as I know—to collect under one cover all the Egyptian objects which have been found in the Aegean area down to the close of the XXVIth Dynasty.

I had intended to include Rhodes, but have been dissuaded therefrom by two facts. Firstly, it would entirely outbalance the rest of the book (there are some 1500 objects from there). Secondly, the Italian excavations of Ialysos, the first scientific excavations yet attempted on the island, are soon to be published, and I hope to show in the report, which Professor Maiuri of Naples has done me the honour of accepting, the importance of the Egyptian finds as supplementing the mass of material lying with context unknown in the British Museum,[1] and as showing beyond doubt how Rhodes alone of the Aegean lands kept up close contact with Egypt throughout every period from the Late Bronze Age.

I must meanwhile thank Dr Jacopi, Director of the Rhodes Museum, for his courtesy in allowing me full permission to study the finds.

In the present catalogue the difficulties have been twofold: the extraordinary diversity of publications and languages in which the original references are to be found; and the widely scattered state of the objects themselves. Many have never been properly published, or were published in the days when they themselves were the centre of interest apart from where and in what context they were found.

The plan adopted has been to give a short account of each site from the point of view in question, and then to give a catalogue of the objects with their context. The numbering runs right through and the Dynasty is given a prominent place after each object or series of objects.

Tables will be found at the end showing: (1) the objects which can be referred to some definite pottery stratum; (2) the objects which can be referred to each Dynasty; (3) the Museums which contain the objects; (4) the types of objects and their materials; (5) the Kings or Queens who have left their names.

I have also included a list of sites in Egypt where Aegean pottery has been found, though the details of this I hope to work out with my wife in another volume.

---

[1] The most important objects in the British Museum are from Tomb 9 at Ialysos, with L.H. III pottery: (1) large scarab of Amenhotep III (1412–1376); (2) smaller scarab of XVIIIth Dynasty, engraved with a "ded" between uraei; (3) small scarab, broken, with a leaf design, also XVIIIth Dynasty (B.M. Vase Room I, Case F. Forsdyke, *J.H.S.* XXXI. p. 114. Furtwängler-Loeschke, *Mykenische Vasen*, Pl. E. Nos. 1–3).

Lastly there are maps, showing the distribution of objects from Egypt in the Aegean, and of objects from the Aegean in Egypt, and an index referring to the text apart from the catalogue.

References have been made as far as possible to works which contain an illustration as well as to the original publication. For my own illustrations I must thank Sir Arthur Evans for permission to use four of the photographs on Plate II (Nos. 25, 26, 28, 30), the British Museum for No. 226 on Plate III and the Fitzwilliam Museum, Cambridge, for No. 227 on the same plate. The rest are of my own taking, except that of the statuette of User on Plate II and the ivory statuettes from Palaikastro on Plate III, both of which were kindly taken for me in my absence by Mr H. G. G. Payne. The drawings in the text are the work of my wife.

In conclusion I wish to thank Mr A. J. B. Wace for suggesting the task and for much invaluable help; Sir Arthur Evans for his hospitality and generous advice when I have been in Crete; Dr H. R. Hall who has kindly read through my work and corrected it in many places; Dr H. Frankfort who introduced me to the practical side of Egyptology and Mr S. R. K. Glanville who has often assisted me in my varied problems; while but for Mr C. T. Seltman I should long ago have despaired of my task.

Also I would like to say how much I appreciate the kindness of Dr Castriotis and the late Dr Xanthoudides in Athens and Candia respectively; and last, but not least, my admiration and thanks are due to the untiring "Phylakes" of many a country and island museum for the long hours they have spent uncomplainingly holding open cases.

J. D. S. P.

1929

FOREWORD

MR PENDLEBURY's collection of all the known ancient Egyptian objects, dating up till the end of the XXVIth Dynasty, from Greek archaeological sites, will be most useful as a book of reference to all students of prehistoric and early Greek archaeology. Its usefulness is enhanced by the careful dating of all the objects described, a work which our knowledge of Egyptian archaeology enables us to do with practical certainty, especially in the important matter of scarabs. In addition to this, Mr Pendlebury's book is of considerable interest as showing us what sort of things from Egypt were prized by the Greeks of the Bronze and Early Iron Ages, and the kind of memento of the Land of the Nile which early Greek seafarers were in the habit of bringing back with them, much as we bring back scarabs and ushabtis ourselves nowadays. There is one difference, however, the ushabti (with a single doubtful exception) does not appear: it was a funerary object that belonged only to the dead in their tombs at a time when Egyptian religion was a living thing, and it did not fall into the hands of a casual tourist as it does now. Figures of gods were in a different category: they could be bought as ordinary objects of worship, and naturally appear exported to Greece. But the scarab, an adornment of the living as well as of the dead, was as popular a memento of Egypt, from the earliest days of its existence at the end of the Old Kingdom (*c.* 2500 B.C.), as it is now. The scarab and the vase of alabaster and faience (more often the former as the more durable) were the common Egyptian things most prized in Greece: the alabastron, no doubt, usually came containing Egyptian unguents, as in return the Minoan "stirrup vase" was exported to Egypt from Greece with olive-oil or some other Greek product in it.

Mr Pendlebury has given us just such a collection of "Aegyptiaca" in Greece as I myself would have liked to compile years ago, but was dissuaded from doing so by lack of time and opportunity to search through the local museums of Greece for material. This Mr Pendlebury has done, with the result that he has provided us with a very complete and acceptable conspectus of the evidence existing up to date. We may hope that he will next give us a similar collection of the "Minoica" and "Mycenaica" in Egypt.

I have read his descriptions of scarabs very carefully, and have made occasional suggestions with regard to the readings of their legends, etc., but I can only congratulate him on the very great knowledge of their styles and inscriptions that he shows, as well as of other sides of Egyptian archaeology.

H. R. HALL

CONTENTS

PLATES & MAPS

The scale is given in every case. Scarabs both in the plates and in the text are always life-size. The vases drawn in the text for Nos. 72, 92–94, 153–156 are to no scale but merely show the shape. An asterisk in the text denotes that an object is illustrated in one of the plates.

PLATES & MAPS

The scale is given in every case. Scarabs both in the plates and in the text are always life-size. The vases drawn in the text for Nos. 72, 92–94, 153–156 are to no scale but merely show the shape. An asterisk in the text denotes that an object is illustrated in one of the plates.

BIBLIOGRAPHY

Die Kretisch-Mykenische Kultur, by D. Fimmen (1922), is a work indispensable to those interested in the subject. It covers a tremendous range and its great value lies in the exhaustive bibliography of each prehistoric site.

For the connections of Egypt and Crete in early times by far the best illustrated and most suggestive work is to be found in the *Palace of Minos* by Sir Arthur Evans. There are also—though they are chiefly concerned with ceramics—the two volumes of Dr H. Frankfort's *Pottery of the Near East*, while his chapter in the *Mural Paintings of el 'Amarneh* is invaluable for its hints as to the influence of Cretan art on Egypt and for its references to the latest literature on the subject. For Egyptian connections with the Mainland one must turn to Dr H. R. Hall's *Civilization of Greece in the Bronze Age*.

These are the general works on the subject. I have attempted no more, because the scattered references which would otherwise be necessary are all to be found under the respective sites.

The following are the abbreviations used:

A.J.A.	*American Journal of Archaeology.*
Arch. Anz.	*Archäologischer Anzeiger* in *Jahrbuch des Deutschen Archäologischen Instituts.*
Arch. Delt.	Ἀρχαιολογικὸν Δέλτιον.
At. Mitt.	*Mittheilungen des Deutschen Archäologischen Instituts, Athenische Abteilung.*
B.C.H.	*Bulletin de Correspondance Hellénique.*
B.S.A.	*Annual of the British School at Athens.*
C.A.H.	*Cambridge Ancient History.*
Cat. Fig. Ant. du Louvre	*Catalogue des Figurines Antiques de Terre Cuite de Musée du Louvre.* Léon Heuzey.
E.E.C.	*Excavations in Eastern Crete, Sphoungaras and Vrokastro.* Miss E. Hall.
Eph. Arch.	Ἐφημερὶς Ἀρχαιολογική.
Fimmen	*Die Kretisch-Mykenische Kultur.*
J.H.S.	*Journal of the Hellenic Society.*
Mon. Ant.	*Monimenti Antichi.*
P. of M.	*Palace of Minos.* Sir Arthur Evans.
P.S.B.A.	*Proceedings of the Society of Biblical Archaeology.*
V.T.M.	*Vaulted Tombs of the Messará.* S. Xanthoudides. (Translated by Professor Droop.)

INTRODUCTION

THE connection of Egypt with the Aegean is of the greatest importance not only in early times when it provides us with our only positive dating, but also all through early Greek history, for it shows us where to turn for possible foreign influence on art and culture.

The following is concerned with the undeniable evidence of archaeological finds, and has some strange facts to show. Single objects may not have much value as evidence. It cannot be maintained that Boeotian Thebes owes anything to Egypt just because a scarab was found in a Theban tomb, any more than that because a few pieces of iron were found in the Kamares Cave the Minoans must have been an iron-using race, or that because a piece of jade was found at Troy the Trojans were in close relations with the Far East. But on the whole the finds do show how far Egyptian influence reached, at what dates and where that influence is to be looked for, and at what dates and where it is totally absent.

One must go cautiously in using the discoveries for dating purposes. Several stone vases of the Old Kingdom have turned up in deposits thousands of years later. Other objects too may have been kept as heirlooms or bought as "genuine antiques" in Egypt itself. Not all the scarabs which bear the name of Thothmes III date from his time. His name was one to conjure with, not only in Egypt but, for hundreds of years after his death, in Syria, where, like Richard Cœur de Lion, he was the bogy of children and the cause of all unknown fear. For Cyprus, too, which he may actually have conquered as he claims, hundreds of scarabs bearing his name were made as amulets more than a thousand years later.

As is shown in more detail below,[1] Predynastic Egypt has left its mark on the south of Crete and two objects at least have found their way north to Knossos.

Objects of the Old Kingdom, i.e. Dynasties I–VI, are found in the Messarà Plain, at Knossos, and in the east of the island at Mokhlos. The stone bowls of Mycenae and Asine can be omitted for they are well out of their context, though it might be conceivable that they were kept for a long time as heirlooms, since the men of the Mainland had little skill in making such vessels.

The succeeding dynasties are a blank save for a few rough scarabs. Egypt was in the grip of a barons' war for some hundreds of years. There was a foreign domination by Syrians. Even the stronger Kings, like Khety, merely held tight to the throne. The seal-stones of the "double sickle" pattern, however, found at Mokhlos and

[1] Introduction to Crete.

elsewhere, seem to show some common source with similar examples belonging to the First Intermediate Period in Egypt.[1]

With the Middle Kingdom, i.e. Dynasties XI, XII and XIII, again the finds carry us no farther than Crete, though there the influence on art was intense. The Messarà Plain, Pyrgos on the road north, Knossos, Gournes on the north coast, and the sacred Dictaean Cave in the heart of the mountains are the scenes of discovery. The potter's wheel, faience, and certain designs for gems, are Egypt's gifts.[2]

Then again the curtain falls on the tragedy of the Hyksos. Once only it rises: at Knossos we find an alabaster lid of the greatest Hyksos King—Khyan. Otherwise Dynasties XIV–XVII are blank.

Then comes the great revival of the XVIIIth Dynasty. Egypt carves herself a huge Empire and traces of her spread all over the Aegean world. In Crete are found alabaster vases, scarabs, beads and amulets. Agia Triada, Kalyvia the necropolis of Phaestos, the tombs of Knossos (not the Palace, strangely), and the Dictaean Cave, have provided us with results useful to our purpose. In Laconia, at Vaphio, vases are found. In the Argolid, Mycenae had objects of Amenhotep II, Amenhotep III and his wife Tiyi, as well as many fragments of alabaster and faience; the Heraeum also produces a scarab and a vase from its tombs; there is an alabaster vase from Midea—the modern Dendra—where the great rich tholos was found: there are jars from Menidi in Attica and an alabaster vase from Chalcis in Euboea.[3] The period of the XIXth Dynasty is chiefly remarkable for the fact that Greece has preserved no record of Rameses II, whose output of scarabs in his own country was only rivalled by the number of his buildings and his children. He sought to make it as if no other Pharaoh had ever reigned, yet his name seems to be unknown in the Aegean. Crete, now under the Achaean domination,[4] disappears apparently from the Egyptian view. Perhaps the Egyptians thought it had disappeared literally, and invented the Atlantis legend. But Laconia, the Argolid, and Thebes in Boeotia still provide objects.

Then again comes a blank, but this time only in history. During the dark ages in

---

[1] The source is almost certainly Anatolian, see Frankfort, *J.E.A.* XII. p. 80 ff., and for the whole of the First Intermediate Period; and for this class of seals in Crete, see *P. of M.* I. pp. 123, 124.

[2] See *P. of M.* I. p. 201. The wheel however has probably its ultimate origin in Sumeria. See Hall, *Civilization of Greece in the Bronze Age*, p. 84.

[3] There are two more objects of this period which I have not included in the catalogue. They are both frog amulets of the type so frequently found at Amarna (cf. Petrie, *Tell el Amarna*, Pl. XVII. No. 328); one in my possession is said to be from Thasos, one in the possession of Mr Seltman is said to be from Aegina. The provenance of neither is certain enough to warrant inclusion.

[4] How much of Cretan culture the Achaeans destroyed and how much they took over can hardly be determined until more sites, such as Arkades, are excavated. Was the Minoan thalassocracy destroyed and were the cities of Crete sacked in order to open up the Egyptian trade for the men of the Mainland? This would explain the sudden influx of Egyptian objects into the Mainland and of Mainland objects into Egypt which suddenly begins in the middle of the reign of Amenhotep III. I hope to enlarge on this theme elsewhere.

Greece there were plenty of opportunities to collect "souvenirs" of a successful raid or even of a peaceful visit. The art—if it can be so called—of the XXth to XXVth Dynasties appears in Crete at Arkades up in the Lasithi Mountains, at Vrokastro on the Hierapetra Peninsula, and at Kavousi in the east. At Sparta scarabs were found in the oldest deposit in the Sanctuary of Artemis Orthia. At Athens in the Dipylon Cemetery and on the Acropolis, and at Eleusis in tombs and outside the oldest Telesterion, objects have turned up. Even in Thessaly a bronze vase and, they say, scarabs[1] have appeared.

The XXVIth Dynasty is in sheer force of numbers the most productive of Egyptian objects in the Aegean world. It was perhaps lucky for the Greeks that the really close connections which they had with Egypt at that time should happen to be during a very fine artistic outburst. In this dynasty Egypt attempted, and to a large extent succeeded in, the amazing device of putting back the artistic clock nearly 3000 years. In art, literature and official life they went right back to the Old Kingdom, and, astounding as it may seem, they did to a great extent succeed in recapturing some of the wonderful freshness of that period. Then too, as never before, the ordinary Greek, not the adventurer alone, had the opportunity of visiting Egypt. There was the great trading station at Naucratis and, for all we know, personally conducted tours up the Nile by guides as delightfully inaccurate as their descendants. A possible result of this throwing open of a hitherto forbidden land I have suggested below;[2] the visible outcome can be seen in the hundreds of scarabs and figurines in faience, which were found in great hoards in Greece. The Menelaion near Sparta, the Argive Heraeum, Corinth, Athens, Sunium, Aegina, are all well represented.

With the close of the XXVIth Dynasty Egypt, except for short, desperately troubled periods, was never again a free country, and here our story ends.

In conclusion it may be interesting to see some of the places in which no Egyptian object has been found. Among these I put Western Crete[3] very tentatively. The Canea and Rhethymno Museums have an Egyptian collection, but absence of a museum inventory and lack of all record makes it uncertain whether any of the objects were found in Crete at all.

More surprising is the total absence of finds at Olympia and Delphi. Though this may perhaps be accounted for by the fact that the excavators here, as at Corinth, have not yet reached a low enough level, it is nevertheless surprising.

But Crete, the bridge between Europe and Africa, is well represented in almost every period, while, after the XVIIIth Dynasty, Laconia, the Argolid, Attica are never out of touch with Egypt.

[1] We await Dr Arvanitopoulos' report of an excavation too many years old.
[2] See Introduction to Aegina, p. 95.
[3] But see *Eph. Arch.* 1907, p. 163, Pl. VI. No. 42, for a seal said to come from Eleutherna and resembling those from Vrokastro. Candia Museum, Inventory No. 64.

CRETE

CRETE

THE importance of the contacts between Egypt and Crete cannot be over-emphasized. For one thing, they give the only positive and absolute dates which can be assigned to the Minoan Periods. Although Egyptologists may still be quarrelling over the dates of the earlier dynasties, yet every year they are getting nearer to an agreement, and already by well-nigh universal consent the beginning of the XIIth Dynasty is dated to *c.* 2200 (Hall) or 2000 (Meyer) and with it the Middle Minoan II Period. The Old Kingdom chronology is still in dispute, but there is now little doubt that the Ist Dynasty is to be placed soon after the middle of the fourth millenium B.C.[1]

The discoveries of the last few years have somewhat disturbed the easy old equation—IVth Dynasty = Early Minoan II, XIIth Dynasty = Middle Minoan II, XVIIIth Dynasty = Late Minoan II—but not seriously.

The connection of Egypt with Crete possibly begins in the days when King Menes[2] conquered the north of Egypt. Some of the inhabitants fled, crossed the sea and settled in the fertile Messarà Plain: hence the ivory figures, etc.[3] It is they who may have started the Bronze Age in Southern Crete.[4]

Dr Frankfort[5] holds that the east of Crete was in advance of the centre (i.e. Knossos) owing to the early advent of bronze from Anatolia. It is hardly possible to deny that the south was also in advance. Knossos was still in the Stone Age when early dynastic vessels appear.

Here perhaps is the place for a statement reiterated later. Egyptian stone vessels in Crete are much better evidence than those found on the mainland. That is to say, wherever they are found they may be used for dating.[6] This was in all probability due to the fact that the Cretans were great workers in stone themselves. Steatite and porphyry, liparite and serpentine were easily obtainable, as well as marble and the curious variegated stones of Mokhlos. Therefore they were unlikely to treasure the Egyptian specimens as did the inhabitants of the mainland.

So much for the Stone Age and Early Minoan Period, though it may be remarked in passing that no Cretan work of this time has appeared in Egypt. The First Inter-

---

[1] Cf. however Scharff in *J.E.A.* XVIII. p. 275, for arguments for a lower date and his references there.

[2] Dr Hall considers it to have been a much more gradual affair, for Menes is probably a composite figure including Narmer and Aha. He points out that the connections with the Delta, though considerable, are not sufficient to justify so convenient an assumption.

[3] See below under Platanos. These figures, however, are considerably later in date than their prototypes.

[4] See *P. of M.* II. i. chapter ii for whole period.

[5] See Frankfort, *Asia, Europe and the Aegean, and their Earliest Interrelations*, p. 94.

[6] See below under Knossos and Mycenae. They are however in any case very risky. A Middle Pre-dynastic bowl of the same shape as No. 22 was found at Tell el Amarna in 1929 in a pure late XVIIIth Dynasty deposit.

mediate Period is illustrated by rude scarabs at Marathokephalon and Platanos, Agia Triada and Gournes.

The equation of the Middle Minoan Period with the Middle Kingdom in Egypt is however doubly substantiated. Middle Minoan II polychrome pottery with the "racquet-and-ball" pattern—so-called Kamares ware—has been discovered at Lahun, Harageh and Abydos in undoubted XIIth Dynasty contexts.[1] In Crete the discovery of the XIIth Dynasty statue of User at Knossos, and of a Middle Kingdom scarab at Platanos, both in Middle Minoan deposits, put the matter beyond doubt. In addition is the curious fact that during the XIIth Dynasty, Amenemhat III—the Lamaris of the Greeks—built the so-called Labyrinth of Hawara, while it was during the Middle Minoan Period that the Labyrinths of Crete—the great Palaces of Knossos and Phaestos—were begun.[2]

The transition period was a troubled one in both countries. The Hyksos horde overran Egypt; Crete seems to have suffered from a severe earthquake which certainly destroyed much of the Palace of Knossos. Then comes the splendid dawn of the Empire in Egypt and the Late Minoan Period in Crete, an age, on both sides, of magnificence, not perhaps comparable with the simpler and more tasteful periods before, but nevertheless very imposing. During this time intercourse between the two countries was very close. We hear of the Keftians;[3] they are seen bearing gifts to Thothmes III—tribute he called it. The alabaster vases, scarabs and beads of the XVIIIth Dynasty become common all over Crete. The name of Tiyi, wife of Amenhotep III, has found its way to Agia Triada; the great prince buried in the Royal Tomb at Isopata must needs have many Egyptian vases for his welfare after death.

There is only one real difficulty: How is it that no Late Minoan II pottery has been found in Egypt? Perhaps the answer is that Late Minoan II was only a local blaze at Knossos, and that no other part of Crete was affected.[4] This will also explain why at Phaestos, at Agia Triada and at Gournia the Late Minoan III Period follows almost immediately on Late Minoan I.

Crete fell before the Achaeans.[5] Perhaps the fine craftsmen fled to Egypt and found refuge at Akhenaten's court, there to enliven the painters and potters.[6] Perhaps they added that touch of informality which is the key-note of the reign.

In return we have nothing, until the Achaeans are overthrown in their turn and Crete is in the throes of the Geometric Age. Then the adventurers and the pirates

[1] See Petrie, *Illahun, Kahun and Gurob*; Engelbach and Gunn, *Harageh*.
[2] See below under Knossos, and H. R. Hall in *J.H.S.* xxv. p. 320 ff.
[3] For an attack on the identification of the Keftians with Crete see Wainwright in *Liverpool Annals*, vi. p. 24. General opinion however is still in favour of the Keftians being at any rate mainly Cretans.
[4] See *P. of M.* i. p. 29.
[5] See above, p. xviii, note 4.
[6] For their influence see Frankfort in *Mural Paintings of El 'Amarneh*, chapter i.

may have brought back the scarabs and faience found in the tombs of their chieftains at Arkades, Kavousi and Vrokastro.

In conclusion, the Predynastic peoples may have entered the Messarà and brought their culture to the south. The Old Kingdom reaches the Messarà, Knossos and Mokhlos. The Middle Kingdom finds the route from the Messarà *via* Pyrgos to Knossos and to the sacred Dictaean Cave. It leaves its mark on Gournes. The New Empire can be traced at Agia Triada, Kalyvia near Phaestos, and at the tombs of Knossos, and a statuette of the period is dedicated long after in the Dictaean Cave; while Egypt of the decadence from the XXth to the XXVIth Dynasty was plundered for the objects of Arkades, Kavousi and Vrokastro.

I. AGIOS ONOUPHRIOS

A large heap of human bones and skulls, the débris of a series of interments, was discovered at Agios Onouphrios on the south slope of a hill about a quarter of a mile north of Phaestos. The burials seem to date from the late Early Minoan Period, but continue into Middle Minoan.

AGIOS ONOUPHRIOS

*1. *Scarab.*

Amethyst. Three circles, probably to be covered with gold leaf. (Plate I.)   *XIIth DYNASTY*

*2. *Scarab.*

White steatite. Six circles. (Cf. Petrie, *Gizeh and Rifeh*, Pl. XXIII. No. 15.) (Plate I.)

XIIth DYNASTY

*3. *Scarab.*

White steatite. Spiral decoration within a border. (Plate I.)

XIIth DYNASTY

*4. *Scarab.*

Paste. Inscription—Amen-Ra Neb Pet (?) (Amen-Ra, Lord of the Sky). Bad and careless writing. (Cf. Petrie, *Illahun, Kahun and Gurob*, Pl. XXIII. No. 73.) (Plate I.)

XVIIIth DYNASTY

*5. *Scarab.*

Onyx. Lotus(?) (Cf. Brunton, *Qau and Badari*, I. Pl. XXXIII. No. 191.) (Plate I.)

Context: seal-stones, marble figures of Amorgos type, bronze daggers, bronze lamps covered with gold leaf, gold rings, E.M. pottery.

(Candia Museum. Middle case 58, Nos. 45, 44, 46, 48, 47. Evans, *Cretan Pictographs* (Supplement), p. 105 ff.)

XIIth DYNASTY

II. AGIA TRIADA

The site of a Palace and adjoining houses dating chiefly from the Late Minoan I Period. From the Palace itself only one object has come, though the excavators claim two stone bowls found with it as Egyptian in spite of the fact that the material of which they are made is not Egyptian.

In a large domed tomb about five minutes east of the Palace two scarabs and an amulet have come to light, and in a chamber-tomb situated inside an older house was discovered the most important object of all, the scarab of Queen Tiyi, wife of Amenhotep III of the XVIIIth Dynasty, 1412–1376 B.C.

The tholos of course belongs to the series discovered in the Messarà Plain and dating from Early Minoan times; the finds in the Palace and the chamber-tomb only confirm our knowledge of the Late Minoan I–II Period.

AGIA TRIADA

LARGE THOLOS

*6. *Scarab.*
White paste. Insect (?) engraved. (Cf. Platanos, No. 55, and Brunton, *Qau and Badari*, I. Pl. XXXIV. No. 199.) (Plate I.)

FIRST INTERMEDIATE PERIOD

*7. *Circular Seal.*
White paste. Lotus design. (Cf. Petrie and Quibell, *Naqada and Ballas*, Pl. LXXX. No. 71.) (Plate I.)

EARLY XIIth DYNASTY

8. *Ape Amulet.*
Lapis lazuli. Squatting. 2·5 cms. high. (Cf. Engelbach and Gunn, *Harageh*, Pl. L. κ.)

Context: vessels and implements of clay and stone, stone seals, ivory figures, gold leaf, beads, E.M. II–III pottery.

(Candia Museum. Middle case 36, Nos. 1024, 1020 and unnumbered. *Memorie del Reale Istituto Lombardo*, XXI. pp. 248–251, Pls. VII–XI.)

XIIth DYNASTY

PALACE

9. *Vase.*
Baggy vase of banded alabaster 20·0 cms. high. (Cf. below, Isopata, Nos. 35, 36.)

Context: two stone bowls of Egyptian shape but Cretan material. L.M. I pottery.

(*Ibid.* Middle case 39, No. 343. *Mon. Ant.* XIII. p. 62.)

XVIIIth DYNASTY

CHAMBER-TOMB

*10. *Circular Seal.*
White steatite (found in chamber-tomb 5 in old house southeast of Palace). Tiyi, wife of Amenhotep III, 1412–1376 B.C. "Royal Wife Tiyi." (Plate I.)

Context: bronze daggers, gold necklet, bull's head pendant, Bucchero vase, L.M. I–II pottery.

(*Ibid.* Middle case 39, No. 340. *Mon. Ant.* XIV. p. 735.)

AMENHOTEP III, XVIIIth DYNASTY

9

III. ARKADES (APHRATI)

Arkades is the site of the ancient Arcadia and lies about thirty miles to the south-east of Candia in the Lasithi Mountains. Here the Italians discovered a very interesting settlement dating from apparently the tenth century B.C. On the western terrace were discovered several tholoi, constructed of large, carefully squared stones and built in Achaean times, though subsequently cleared and used by the late comers.

The settlement is particularly interesting as being one of the few discovered in Crete which shed any light on the civilization of the island in very early Hellenic times.

The objects in question all come from the largest tholos on the western terrace.

I am indebted to Professor Halbherr for permission to make use of these objects.

ARKADES (APHRATI)

11. *Small Bowl.*

Blue faience. 7·5 cms. across widest part. Encrusted surface. Two zones of decoration: on the upper, lions pursuing stags; on the lower, bulls grazing and charging.

(Candia Museum. Centre case 79 Γ, unnumbered.)

XXIst—XXIInd DYNASTIES

*12. *Scarab.*

Brownish paste. Rude figure holding a crocodile in either hand. (Cf. Newberry, *Catalogue of Scarabs in the Cairo Museum*, Pl. X. No. 36,372.) (Plate I.)

(*Ibid.* Wall case 79 A, No. 1309.)

XIXth—XXIInd DYNASTIES

*13. *Scarab.*

White paste. Hawk with double crown. Uraeus. Horned moon. Ankh sign of life. Feather. (Cf. Newberry, *Catalogue of Scarabs in the Cairo Museum*, Pl. VI. No. 36,490.) (Plate I.)

Context: necklaces, gold leaf, bronze pins, swords and spear-blades, decadent L.M. III pottery, Geometric and proto-Corinthian.

(*Ibid.* No. 1310. *Liverpool Annals*, 1925, pp. 3–14, Pl. II *b*.)

XIXth—XXIInd DYNASTIES

IV. DICTAEAN CAVE (PSYKHRO)

The Dictaean Cave is situated above the upland plain of Psykhro in the Lasithi Mountains about fifteen minutes' climb from the village of Psykhro. It was a place for sacred offerings from Middle Minoan times until the beginning of the eighth century, for the pottery begins with a small deposit of Kamares ware and ends in good Geometric times without a trace of Oriental influence. The excavators suggest that its associations may then have been moved to the Idaean Cave.

The cave consists of an upper and a lower grotto, in the latter of which, from the mud at the bottom, the statuette No. 15 was extracted.

14. *Scarab.*

Amethyst. A rayed sun between two beaked vases. Circles in the field. Probably engraved by a Minoan artist. Found in cave long before the excavations. No context.

(In the possession of Sir Arthur Evans. *Scripta Minoa*, p. 136; *P. of M.* 1. p. 199.)   *XIIth DYNASTY*

*15. *Bronze Statuette.*

Amen-Ra, with double plume. 10 cms. high. Good New Empire work. Dedicated about 900 B.C. Found in mud at bottom of lower grotto. (Frontispiece.)

Context: rude bronze figures, rings, pins, double axes, gems with animals engraved, e.g. heraldic goats, lions, etc.

(Candia Museum. Wall case 1, No. 422. *B.S.A.* VI. p. 107, Pl. X.)

XVIIIth—XIXth DYNASTIES

V. GOURNES

A small site some two miles inland about seven and a half miles east of Candia. Here in 1915 Hazzidakis discovered several burial enclosures built of rough stones. Large quantities of Early Minoan pottery came to light and a number of seal-stones of the same date. The finds are really to be taken in conjunction with those of the Messarà Plain rather than with anything in the north.

GOURNES

16. *String of Beads.*

Faience. Some cylindrical XIIth Dynasty type. Some oval. (Candia Museum. Wall case 64, No. 1237.)

XIIth DYNASTY

*17. Scarab.

From Tomb B. White steatite. Criss-cross pattern. (Cf. for pattern Brunton, *Qau and Badari*, 1. Pl. XXXIII. No. 156. Mr Brunton however is uncertain about this specimen from Gournes.) (Plate I.)

(*Ibid.* No. 1184.)

FIRST INTERMEDIATE PERIOD

*18. Scarab.

From the same tomb. White steatite. Spiral decoration. (Cf. Petrie, *Illahun, Kahun and Gurob*, Pl. VIII. Nos. 68 and 71.) (Plate I.)

Context: E.M. III pottery. E.M. seal-stones. Terracotta female statuette with " caul " headdress.

(*Ibid.* Unnumbered. *Arch. Delt.* 1915, p. 60; 1918, pp. 55, 56, Pls. IV, V.)

EARLY XIIth DYNASTY

VI. KALYVIA

Between Phaestos and the village of Kalyvia. A necropolis consisting of several Late Minoan tombs, some excavated by Xanthoudides in 1901, so far unpublished; some by the Italians in 1902–1904. It was evidently the burial-place of the settlement at Phaestos, for there is one magnificent royal tomb. The chamber-tomb in which these vases were found was evidently used and re-used, for the pottery extends over the whole of the Late Minoan Period.

KALYVIA

19. *Alabaster Vase.*

Found in chamber-tomb 4. A baggy vase of banded alabaster. 49·5 cms. high. (Cf. below, Isopata, Nos. 35, 36.)

(Candia Museum. Middle case 45, No. 175.)

XVIIIth DYNASTY

20. *Alabaster Vase.*

Found in the same tomb. Baggy, but with a short cylindrical neck. 18 cms. high.

Context: L.M. I–II–III vases.

(*Ibid.* No. 46. *Mon. Ant.* XIV. p. 554.)

XVIIIth DYNASTY

VII. KAVOUSI

The village of Kavousi lies on a spur of Mt Aphendi Kavousi, which cuts right across the island to the east of the Isthmus of Hierapetra. It is about an hour's walk from Pakhyammos, the nearest port of call for ships. Here in 1900 Miss Boyd discovered a settlement and several tholos and chamber-tombs, dating both from Minoan and Geometric times. It is curious that this settlement alone of those which lie across the Isthmus of Hierapetra, Vasiliki, Pakhyammos and Gournia, should provide us with anything Egyptian. As the French found during the Cretan revolution, the isthmus provided a much cheaper, safer, and quicker way of transport than the sea route round the east coast. Hierapetra is almost the best port from the point of view of the Egyptian trade, and it is probably only because no thorough excavation has been attempted there that no evidence has come to light, but even that does not account for its absence in such thoroughly dug sites as the other three mentioned.

KAVOUSI

21. *Fragment of Faience.*   Since perished.

Context: iron sword blades, fine Geometric pottery. Oriental influence beginning to show on thin bronze plate.

(*A.J.A.* 1901, p. 146.)

PROBABLY THIRD INTERMEDIATE PERIOD

VIII. KNOSSOS

The connection of Knossos with Egypt goes back to the Neolithic Age and extends right down through every period to the end of Minoan times. The Neolithic Era is the richest in evidence, for more and more fragments of stone vases are turning up every day. The finds from this stratum seem to be mainly Predynastic, but one at least (No. 26) belongs to the Early Dynastic Period, Dynasties I–II. In a pure Early Minoan stratum we find nothing. That is owing to the fact that nearly all the Early Minoan deposit was swept off the top of the site to make room for the earliest Palace. The resulting débris was dumped chiefly in the north-western area; but it is probably from this Early Minoan stratum that the porphyry bowls Nos. 22, 23 and 25 originally came. In late Middle Minoan times two very important finds appear, Nos. 29 and 30. The diorite statue of the Egyptian official User is interesting when we remember that at the same time as the First Palace or Labyrinth was being constructed at Knossos, King Amenemhat III, Ne-maat-Ra, or as the Greeks called him, Lamaris, was building his labyrinth in the Fayum.[1] The alabastron lid of Khyan is important as confirming the view that this King was well known outside Egypt; a lion with his name was found at Baghdad. Alone of the Hyksos usurpers has he left any trace of himself or his period except in Egypt.

The Late Minoan contacts are confined to the tombs at Isopata and Zafer Papoura. The Egyptian objects all date from the XVIIIth Dynasty with one exception, and are all found in suitable contexts, as indeed is usually the case with all but stone vases, though these in Crete do not seem to have passed as heirlooms in the same way as on the mainland, perhaps because the Cretans were themselves fine workers in stone.

[1] See *J.H.S.* xxv. p. 320 ff.

KNOSSOS

PALACE

22. Hornblende Porphyry Bowl.

Found in the unstratified deposit north-west of Palace site. 20 cms. across mouth. 11 cms. high. Flat, finely undercut collar. Perforated roll handles broken off. Cf. Mycenae, No. 95.

(Candia Museum. Side case 23 a, No. 2092. *P. of M.* II. i. p. 30, fig. 12 (restored).)

MIDDLE PREDYNASTIC (sequence date 45–54)

23. Hornblende Porphyry Bowl.

Found in same deposit as above, No. 22. Smaller than No. 22. Lower part only. Flat moulded base. Incised ring internally, caused by tubular drill.

(Not yet in Museum. *P. of M.* II. i. p. 31, fig. 28.)

MIDDLE PREDYNASTIC (sequence date 45–54)

24. Diorite Mace Head.

Pear-shaped. Only half remaining. Stratification unknown. (Cf. Petrie, *Prehistoric Egypt*, Pl. XXVI. No. 38.)

(Ashmolean Museum. Case 1. 35, No. 838.)

LATE PREDYNASTIC

*25. Hornblende Porphyry Bowl.

Found in dumped earth north-west of Palace. 15 cms. across the mouth. Much worn. No trace of handles. Lip stands up but is not undercut. (Cf. Garstang, *Mahasna and Bet Khallaf*, Pl. XXIV. K. 4.) (Plate II.)

(*Ibid.* Case 1. 31, No. 201. *P. of M.* I. p. 65, fig. 32.)

Ist—IInd DYNASTIES

*26. Syenite Vessel.

Found inside the south propylaea under the west wing of the Palace. 12 cms. across mouth. 11 cms. high. Flat collar. Ledge handles unperforated. (Cf. Petrie, *Meydum and Memphis* (III), Pl. XIX. No. 7.) (Plate II.)

Context: Neolithic and Sub-Neolithic pottery.

(Candia Museum. Wall case 31, No. 263. *P. of M.* I. p. 65, figs. 28, 31.)

Ist—IInd DYNASTIES

*27. Shallow Diorite Bowl.

Found wedged in south wall of store room of earliest period later Palace. Translucent diorite, carinated outline strongly resembling bowl from tomb of Sneferu. Fragmentary but restored. About 13 cms. across. (Cf. Quibell, *El Kab*, Pl. III. No. 2.) (Plate II.)

Context: a similar but more carinated bowl of liparite, evidently an imitation in liparite, a material only found in the Aeolian Islands, and false spouted jars. M.M. III.

(*Ibid.* Side case 31, No. 590. *P. of M.* I. p. 86, fig. 55 *b*.)

Ist—IVth DYNASTIES

*28. Diorite "Moustache Cup".

Originally 9 cms. high. Found in an unstratified deposit west of the Palace. (Cf. Quibell, *El Kab*, Pl. X. No. 20.) (Plate II.)

(*Ibid.* Side case 31, No. 2170. *P. of M.* II. i. p. 54, fig. 27.)

IVth DYNASTY

*29. *Diorite Statue of User.*

Found to the north-west of the central court. Lower half only of man seated on throne clad in a short kilt of which outline may be seen above knees. Dated by Evers, *Staat aus dem Stein*, II. p. 96, to Amenemhat I. Dr Hall however reads the name as "Ab-nub-mes-wazet-user" and therefore dates it to the early XIIIth Dynasty. Height 12·5 cms.

Inscriptions run:

Back: Devoted to the Great God, Lord of Heaven, Heart of Gold whom the Wazet Nome produced, User, the justified [i.e. deceased].

Sides: The Devoted Heart of Gold whom the Wazet Nome produced, User, the justified, born of the devoted Sat-Hathor, the justified. (Plate II.)

Context: M.M. II *b* pottery.

(Candia Museum. Middle case 20, No. 95. *P. of M.* I. p. 286, fig. 220; II. i. p. 220.)

XIIth DYNASTY

*30. *Lid of Alabastron.*

Found near the north-west lustral basin in M.M. III *a* deposit. Inscribed with the name of the Hyksos King Khyan, 18th century B.C. (?), "The good god, Se-User-en-Ra. Son of the Sun Khyan". (Plate II.)

(*Ibid.* Middle case 16, No. 263. *P. of M.* I. p. 419, fig. 304 *b*.)

XVth DYNASTY

VIII *a*. THE ROYAL TOMB AT ISOPATA

The tomb is situated about two miles north of the Palace. It is a rectangular vaulted structure approached by a long dromos which leads into a narrow fore-hall, on either side of which are two large niches. In the north-east corner of the tomb is a grave-pit in the form of a double axe. The tomb seems to have been in use for a considerable period after its construction, probably at the end of Late Minoan I or the beginning of Late Minoan II.

31. *Two Fragments of Diorite Bowl.* Originally 11 cms. in diameter. (Cf. Quibell, *El Kab*, Pl. X. pp. 17, 30.)

(Candia Museum. Middle case 19. Unnumbered. *Prehistoric Tombs*, fig. 128.)

Ist—IVth DYNASTIES

32. *One-handled Vase.* 25·3 cms. high. Coarse alabaster. (Cf. MacIver and Mace, *El Amrah and Abydos*, Pl. L. Tomb D. 11.)

(*Ibid.* No. 600.)

MID-XVIIIth DYNASTY

33. *Baggy Vase.* 18·5 cms. high. Banded alabaster. (Cf. Petrie and Brunton, *Sedment*, I. Pl. XL. No. 20.)

(*Ibid.* No. 601.)

SECOND INTERMEDIATE PERIOD

34. *Baggy Vase.* 10·5 cms. high. Banded alabaster. (Cf. Petrie and Brunton above, *loc. cit.*)

(*Ibid.* No. 602.)

SECOND INTERMEDIATE PERIOD

*35. *Baggy Vase.* 7·8 cms. high. Banded alabaster. One side broken. (Cf. vase from group in the Ashmolean Museum. Tomb Δ 15 at Abydos.) (Plate III.)

(*Ibid.* No. 603.)

XVIIIth DYNASTY

*36. *Baggy Vase.* 5·4 cms. high. Banded alabaster. Restored. (Cf. vase from group in the Ashmolean Museum. Tomb E 288 at Abydos.) (Plate III.)

(*Ibid.* No. 604.)

XVIIIth DYNASTY

*37. *Vase.* 11·4 cms. high. Cylindrical neck. No foot. Wavy grained alabaster. (Plate III.)

(*Ibid.* No. 605.)

XVIIIth DYNASTY

38. *Vase.* 9·8 cms. high. Similar to above but with shorter neck. Banded alabaster. (Cf. Garstang, *El Arabah*, Pl. XVIII. Tomb E 294.)

(*Ibid.* No. 606.)

XVIIIth DYNASTY

*39. *Vase.* 9·7 cms. high. Globular body. Cylindrical neck. Short foot. Banded alabaster. (Cf. MacIver and Mace, *El Amrah and Abydos*, Pl. XLVI. Tomb D. 116.) (Plate III.)

(*Ibid.* No. 607.)

XVIIIth DYNASTY

40. *Bowl.*

20 cms. across. 8 cms. high. Banded alabaster. Flat base with a round opening about 4 cms. in diameter. A round perforation about half-way down the side.

(*Ibid.* No. 608.)

XVIIIth DYNASTY

41. *Basin.*

19 cms. across. 10·4 cms. high. Banded alabaster. (Cf. Engelbach and Gunn, *Harageh*, Pl. XLVIII. No. 103.)

(*Ibid.* No. 609.)

XVIIIth DYNASTY

42. *String of Beads.*

Lapis lazuli. Only the simple round beads are Egyptian. The rest are Minoan. (Cf. Brunton and Engelbach, *Gurob*, Pl. XLIV. Y.)

XVIIIth DYNASTY

43. *Crouching Frog Amulet.*

1·8 cms. high. Faience. (Cf. Petrie, *Tell el Amarna*, Pl. XVII. No. 328.)

XVIIIth DYNASTY

44, 45. *Two Squatting Apes.*

1·9 cms. high. Lapis lazuli. (Cf. Brunton and Engelbach, *Gurob*, Pl. XLII. M.)

Context: Minoan porphyry bowl. Lamps of purple gypsum with coils in relief. L.M. II pottery.

(*Ibid.* No. 146. Reference for all the above, Evans, *Prehistoric Tombs*, p. 146.)

XVIIIth DYNASTY

A TOMB ON THE SAME PLATEAU

46. *Baggy Vase.*

9 cms. high. Banded alabaster. (Cf. above, Nos. 35, 36.)

Context: bronze swords, axes, bowls, a "talent" weight. L.M. III pottery.

(*Ibid.* Middle case 26, No. 1583.)

XVIIIth DYNASTY

VIII *b*. TOMB AT ZAFER PAPOURA

A series of chamber-tombs, some very large and elaborate, was found on the ridge of Zafer Papoura about half-way between Isopata and Knossos.

*47. *Scarab.*

Found in Tomb 99. White steatite. Nekhebet (the winged snake goddess). Hawk to the right and "nefer" (= good or beautiful). (Cf. Petrie, *Tell el Amarna*, Pl. XV. No. 145.) (Plate I.)

Context: jewellery, small stirrup vases, L.M. III cups, etc.

(Candia Museum. Middle case 27, No. 687. Evans, *Prehistoric Tombs*, p. 89.)

END OF XVIIIth DYNASTY

IX. MARATHOKEPHALON

A small village lying about seven miles north-east of Phaestos, where Xanthoudides in 1918 discovered the remains of a tholos tomb of the Early Minoan Period. The tholos seems to have been used throughout the period.

Like Agia Triada, Platanos, Koumasa, etc., it belongs to the era which follows the assumed North Egyptian immigration at the end of the Predynastic Age.

*48. *Circular Seal.*

Found in the tholos. White steatite. Coil pattern. (Cf. Petrie, *Buttons and Design Scarabs*, Pl. II. No. 74.) (Plate I.)

(Candia Museum. Middle case 58, unnumbered.)

EARLY FIRST INTERMEDIATE PERIOD

*49. *Scarab.*

Found in the tholos. White steatite. Pattern of running triangles. (Cf. Brunton, *Qau and Badari*, 1. Pl. XXXIII. No. 183. Mr Brunton however is uncertain about this specimen from Marathokephalon.) (Plate I.)

Context: bronze daggers, a bead necklace, E.M. pottery of all dates.

(*Ibid.* No. 1227. *Arch. Delt.* 4. 1918, Supplement, p. 21, fig. 7.)

FIRST INTERMEDIATE PERIOD

X. MOKHLOS

A tiny island two hundred yards from the coast below the village of Sphaka and about two miles south-east of Pseira. Here Seager discovered a small settlement and a number of Early Minoan tombs which produced a sensational hoard of jewellery and stone vases. These vases show many affinities with examples of the Old Kingdom in Egypt, but in no case can it be said that there is an actual import.

50. *Fragment of Faience Bowl.*

Found in Tomb VI. So perished that it was impossible to keep. This was one of the finest and least disturbed tombs. It was entered through a sort of mortuary chapel. (Seager, *Explorations in the Island of Mochlos*, p. 54.)

Ist—VIth DYNASTIES (?)

51. *Bead Necklace of Faience.*

Found in Tomb VI. Pear-shaped. Derived from cone-shell beads of Predynastic times.

Context: E.M. II pottery.

(Candia Museum. Middle case 53, unnumbered. *P. of M.* 1. fig. 53.)

Ist—IVth DYNASTIES

XI. PALAIKASTRO

Palaikastro lies at the extreme east of Crete about four hours' walk from Sitia. It has a reasonable harbour and may well—even in Minoan times—have had a rich trade from the sponge fisheries—though in modern days these centre round the other Minoan site of Zakro to the south.

Palaikastro does not seem to have followed the usual course of history of the eastern settlements. Its Early Minoan stratum is negligible and it is from Late Minoan times that its wealth dates.

It was Dr Hall (*Civilization of Greece in the Bronze Age*, p. 273, note) who first pointed out the obviously Egyptian provenance of these figures with their close-cropped hair and their complete nudity. The squatting position of one is exactly paralleled by a Middle Kingdom ivory statuette in the British Museum, and if—as seems probable—they are to be referred to the same date,[1] the fact that they were found with Late Minoan pottery need not worry us when we remember how many other things have been found slightly out of their context (e.g. Nos. 1–5, 90, 226).

They may easily have been brought over in Middle Minoan III; and even such small brittle statuettes could have survived, particularly as there was no disaster at Palaikastro comparable to the earthquake at Knossos.

[1] In spite of their larger size.

PALAIKASTRO

*52. *Ivory Male Figurine.*

Found in same block. 4·3 cms. high. Squatting as if cross-legged, but one leg with the knee raised to the shoulder and the sole of the foot on the ground. Both arms lost. (Cf. B.M. Egyptian Room V. Case F, No. 54,677 (Abydos).) (Plate III.)

Context: Late Minoan pottery of all dates (the exact pottery context is not stated).

(Candia Museum. Case 9, No. 142.)

XIIth DYNASTY

*53. *Ivory Male Figurine.*

Found in block Σ. 8·6 cms. high. Standing, arms to sides. One arm and leg and both feet gone. (Plate III.)

(*Ibid.* Case 9, No. 143. *B.S.A.* Supplement, i (1923), p. 125, Pl. XXVII.)

XIIth DYNASTY

XII. PLATANOS

Platanos lies in the Messarà Plain on the Hieropotamos River some two and a half miles south-west of Gortyna. There were three tholos tombs. In the largest, A, were discovered, as at Koumasa, ivory figures of men with dome-shaped heads, pointed chins and the figure ending in a point, which very much resemble Predynastic Egyptian types from Naqada (*P. of M.* II. i. fig. 13).[1] Tholos B may have been built in Early Minoan III. Middle Minoan I, however, was its main period and further interments were made later.

[1] Dr H. R. Hall was the first to mention these resemblances (*J.E.A.* 1914, p. 113). He considers that they point rather to a common source for both the Cretan and the Egyptian examples than to an importation or even an imitation by Cretans of Egyptian originals.

PLATANOS

*54. *Scarab.*

From Tholos B. White steatite. Coil pattern. (Cf. Petrie, *Illahun, Kahun and Gurob*, Pl. VIII. No. 73.) (Plate I.)

(Candia Museum. Middle case 56, No. 1058.)

XIIth DYNASTY

*55. *Scarab.*

From same tomb. White steatite. Figure of insect with six legs (?). (Cf. Agia Triada, No. 6, and Brunton, *Qau and Badari*, 1. Pl. XXXIV. No. 199.) (Plate I.)

(*Ibid.* No. 1011.)

FIRST INTERMEDIATE PERIOD

*56. *Scarab.*

From same tomb. White steatite. Figure of goddess Taurt and coil pattern. (Plate I.)

Context: Babylonian cylinder, steatite seals, E.M. III–M.M. III pottery—sherds only.

(*Ibid.* No. 1075. Xanthoudides, *V.T.M.* p. 117, Pls. XIV, XV.)

XIIth DYNASTY

XIII. PYRGOS

Pyrgos lies in a commanding position a little south of Khanli Kasteli. It is on the great Minoan road[1] which runs right across Crete from sea to sea.

There are many traces of Minoan work here, and the following were found in a Late Minoan I *a* larnax.

[1] See *P. of M.* II. i. p. 60 ff.

57. *Beads.*

From L.M. I *a* larnax. Amethyst and carnelian, some round, some long. (Cf. Engelbach and Gunn, *Harageh*, Pl. LII. Nos. 73 O and 73 P 2; Pl. LIII. No. 79 P.)

Context: vessel of banded limestone, Mokhlos type, gold ring, Minoan beads.

(Ashmolean Museum, Oxford. Case 1. 36. *P. of M.* II. i. p. 75.)

SECOND INTERMEDIATE PERIOD

XIV. VROKASTRO

A steep hill above the little village of Kalokhorio which lies about a mile from the sea at the south-west corner of the Gulf of Mirabello. Here Miss Hall discovered a small settlement, bone enclosures and chamber-tombs. From one of the latter (Chamber-tomb I on Karakovilia) the following objects appeared, all of which have been paralleled by finds of the XXth—XXIInd Dynasties at Lisht.

58–61. *Four Faience Seals.*

Originally blue. Glaze now entirely disappeared from these and the following, leaving only intensely friable core. Back consists of a pair of shells between which is a perforation.

Engraved: a corruption of "Beloved of Amen."

62, 63. *Two Faience Seals.*

Engraved: a corruption of "Amen-Ra."

64. *Faience Seal.*

Hawk-headed Horus, staff in hand.

65. *String of Beads.*

Carnelian, steatite, faience.

Context: Quasi-Geometric pottery.

(Candia Museum. Wall case 80, unnumbered. E. D. Hall, *E.E.C.* p. 136, Pl. XXXV; H. R. Hall, *Civilization of Greece in the Bronze Age*, p. 263, fig. 342.)

XXth—XXIInd DYNASTIES

XV. UNKNOWN PROVENANCE

66. *Fragment of Diorite Bowl.*

Very thin but not translucent. Recurved rim. Original diameter about 23 cms. (Cf. Petrie and Brunton, *Sedment*, I. Pl. IV. No. 64.)

(Ashmolean Museum, Oxford. Case I. 31.)

Ist—IVth DYNASTIES

*67. *Scarab.*

Green faience, hawk between uraei. (Cf. Petrie, *Kahun, Gurob and Hawara*, Pl. XXIII. No. 113.) (Plate I.)

(Candia Museum. Case 11, No. 51.)

XIXth DYNASTY

*68. *Scarab.*

Glass paste. Amen-Ra (and neter?) (Amen-Ra, the God). (Cf. Petrie, *Kahun, Gurob and Hawara*, Pl. XXIII. No. 81.) (Plate I.)

(*Ibid.* Case 11, No. 52.)

XVIIIth DYNASTY

*69. *Scarab.*

Green faience. Inscription "Neith". (Plate I.)

(*Ibid.* Case 11, No. 121.)

XXVIth DYNASTY

*70. *Scarab.*

Steatite. Female figure within a *bordure componé*. (Cf. Newberry, *Catalogue of Scarabs in the Cairo Museum*, Pl. VII. No. 36,529.) (Plate I.)

(Athens Nat. Museum. Case 67, No. 4679.)

SECOND INTERMEDIATE PERIOD

*71. *Scarab.*

Steatite. Linear pattern. (Cf. Newberry, *Catalogue of Scarabs in the Cairo Museum*, Pl. XIII. Nos. 36,811, etc.) (Plate I.)

(*Ibid.* No. 4680.)

XIXth DYNASTY

LACONIA

XVI. VAPHIO

Vaphio in Laconia is situated about five miles to the south of Sparta in the low hills to the west of the Eurotas. One tholos tomb has been discovered there in a very ruinous condition. It dates probably from Late Helladic II. Its most famous contents are of course the two Vaphio cups of gold repoussé work with figures of oxen, wild and tame.

72. *Pointed Alabaster Amphora.*   Found in the pit in the tholos. 20 cms. high.

XVIIIth—XIXth DYNASTIES

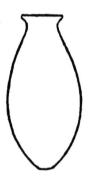

73. *Silver Spoon.*   Found in the preceding. 13 cms. long. Straight handle ending in curl.

LATE XVIIIth—XIXth DYNASTIES

74. *Alabaster Amphora.*   11·7 cms. high. Typical baggy New Empire type. (Cf. Isopata, Nos. 35, 36.)

Context: two gold cups, daggers, steatite lampstand, gold ornaments and rings, seal-stones, etc. L.H. II pottery.

(Athens Nat. Museum. Mycenaean room, Case 88, Nos. 1889, 1876, 1890 respectively. *Eph. Arch.* 1889, pp. 153–154, Pl. VII, figs. 17 and 18.)

XVIIIth DYNASTY

XVII. SPARTA

It is only in the Sanctuary of Artemis Orthia that any Egyptian objects have come to light. This is perhaps natural, since that is the only site which dates from a time when Sparta took the same interest in trade as the rest of the Greek world.

The objects are from the lowest stratum of the sanctuary, and the pottery context is purely Geometric. This places it not later than 750 B.C.

In this case it must be rather the surroundings which date the scarabs than *vice versa*, for with one exception the following works are unfortunately in a very bad condition, which has in some cases precluded strict identification.

Besides these objects, one has only to look through the pages of any work on early Spartan statuettes to see a striking resemblance at first glance to Egyptian examples. This resemblance is chiefly due to the presence of a wig—or it may be some method of dressing the hair which gives a general likeness to the Egyptian wig or striped head-cloth. Whether this is due to a definite Egyptian influence or to mere coincidence it is hard to determine.

Since the above was in print I have been privileged to see the forthcoming full publication of the site. The additional objects from the same stratum will be found on page 109 of this book (immediately after Thera).

75. *Scarab.*

Found in lowest stratum of Sanctuary of Artemis Orthia. Originally covered with blue glaze. Cartouche of Men-kheper-Ra (Thothmes III). The King, wearing the double crown, kneels to the right with his back to the cartouche; by his face is the "ab" sign (= heart); below is the "Neb" sign (= lord).

(Sparta Museum. Store room, Tray 2299. Now almost unrecognizable.)

XXIIIrd—XXVIth DYNASTIES

76. *Large Scarab.*

Found in same stratum as preceding. Paste. Blue glaze gone, very broken, Ra-men (?) nefer-neter hiq—i.e. Ra-men—good God, prince.

(*Ibid.* Room to right, far end case.)

XXIInd—XXVIth DYNASTIES

77. *Paste Figure of Woman.*

Legs gone. Coarse featured, large eyed. A negroid type, much resembling wooden statuettes of negro women of XXIInd—XXVIth Dynasties.

(Sparta Museum (?). Perhaps among other rotting figures in store room, Tray 2286.)

XXIInd—XXVIth DYNASTIES

78, 79. *Two Spindle Whorls.*

Originally blue glaze with daisy pattern in black.

(*Ibid.* Store room, Tray 2218.)

Context for all the above: Geometric pottery of eighth century and ivory plaques of very early type.

(*B.S.A.* XIII. pp. 76 ff. and 88 f.)

XXIInd—XXVIth DYNASTIES

(But see also page 109 for the new material.)

XVIII. MENELAION

The Menelaion, sanctuary of Helen and Menelaus, and perhaps the actual site of the Mycenaean Palace, lies about three miles from Sparta on the other side of the Eurotas, on a conspicuous spur of Therapne. Its remains form a sort of small stepped pyramid, built up round a spur of rock. Round it have been found many remains of Mycenaean houses, but the pyramid itself dates from the latter half of the seventh century at the earliest.

80, 81. *Two Scarabs.*   Paste. Five circles with centres incised.

82. *Scarab.*   Paste. Indecipherable.

83. *Scarab.*   Paste with traces of blue glaze. Lion and sun's disk above.

84. *Scarab.*   Faience. Now much rotted. Indecipherable. Original inscription (from illustration) apparently was a corruption of Neb-Maat-Ra (?). All five are pierced for suspension.

Context: Laconian II pottery and heavy bronze fibulae.

(Sparta Museum. Room to right, Case Γ, Box 1705. *B.S..*. xv. p. 141, Pl. VIII.)

XXVIth DYNASTY

XVIII a. (MISTRA)

There is a little figure in the room to the left of the entrance of the Sparta Museum, Case 2, No. 998. It is 10 cms. high, and is the ushabti of a priestess. Round the figure run texts, but the whole is so worn and dirty that they are almost indecipherable. The original colour, which may have been blue, has now turned to an uneasy black.

The figure was discovered by the "Phylax", Gramarnis, in the hands of a peasant at Mistra—the Byzantine city four miles west of Sparta on a spur of Taygetos— possibly the ancient Harpleia. The man declared that it had been in his family for generations, but he had no knowledge whence it originally came. If this is true it is probably not a forgery, but belongs to the XXVIth Dynasty, though whether it was found at Mistra or Sparta or indeed in Greece at all it is, of course, impossible to say.

ARGOLID

XIX. MYCENAE

There is no legendary, historical or literary tradition of any connection between Mycenae and Egypt if we except the raids of Atreus on Egypt in Mer-en-ptah's reign (1230 B.C.) and of Agamemnon in that of Rameses III (1202 B.C.).[1]

From the finds we see that the contacts are confined to the Empire Period of Egypt and to the great period of Mycenae. In fact we can go closer and say that, with two exceptions, the early and middle XVIIIth Dynasty provides our material.

The first of these exceptions, the fragment of a porphyry bowl—No. 97—found in Tomb No. 518 with Late Helladic I–II pottery, is certainly of Old Kingdom fabric, and together with that found at Asine—No. 149—is an example of the fact that such stone vessels must never be taken as evidence except with the very greatest caution.

The second exception is the fragment of a faience vase—No. 90—found in the third shaft-grave: this, though in a good early Late Helladic I context, cannot be placed before the middle of the XVIIIth Dynasty and much more probably belongs to the XIXth, a period when representations of the Shairdana mercenaries become common.

According to the results of the latest excavations conducted by Wace,[2] the re-building of the Palace, the construction of the Lion Gate and the fortifications, and the building of the third group of tholoi, which includes the Treasury of Atreus and the Tomb of Clytaemnestra (dated by sherds under the threshold and walls of the one, and from an untouched interment in the dromos of the other), should be assigned to the beginning of Late Helladic III. These conclusions are accepted by the German excavators of Tiryns.

Sir Arthur Evans however assigns the Treasury of Atreus and the Tomb of Clytaemnestra to the end of the Middle Helladic Age.[3] His arguments are based on fragments of stone bowls found with Nos. 99 and 100 in the unstratified deep earth which obstructed the dromoi and doorways of these two tombs, and on the likeness of some of the architectural ornament to fragments from Knossos.

A large steatite pithos from the dromos of the Tomb of Clytaemnestra resembles the clay medallion pithoi from Knossos which he dates to Middle Minoan III *b*.[4]

If this dating for the tholoi is correct, it makes them contemporaneous with the shaft-graves. Hence Sir Arthur Evans concludes that the contents of the tholoi were later transferred to the shaft-graves.

There is one other connection. At Tell el Amarna—the city of Akhenaten—there has appeared much pottery of an undeniably Aegean pattern. It is in fact good early

---

[1] Cf. Myres and Frost, *Klio*, 1914, p. 446.
[2] *B.S.A.* xxv. *passim*. *J.H.S.* 1926, p. 110.
[3] See Evans, *The Shaft Graves and Beehive Tombs of Mycenae and their Interrelation*.
[4] But cf. *P. of M.* ii. pp. 320, 562.

Late Helladic III of Rhodian or some similar fabric, closely related to that of the Argolid and not to that of Crete.

Specimens of this type have been found all over Mycenae, particularly in the partially excavated area known as the "Cyclopean Terrace Building".[1] Such sherds have also appeared at other sites in Greece, and its strong likeness to Rhodian and mainland ware,[2] coupled with the fact that the Late Helladic III pottery in Cyprus is of the same type,[3] seems to point to the conclusion that the Amarna sherds are the result of connection between Akhenaten and the mainland, not Crete.

[1] *B.S.A.* xxv. p. 403.
[2] Forsdyke, *Catalogue of Vases in the British Museum*, Vol. I. Part I. p. 183 and references on p. 184.
[3] Gjerstad, *Studies in Prehistoric Cyprus*, p. 325 ff.

MYCENAE

ACROPOLIS

*85. *Blue Faience Ape.*

Cartouche on right shoulder, Aa-kheperu-Ra (Amenhotep II, 1447–1420 B.C.) in yellow. Head and upper part only. Details in white. No context known. (Plate IV.)

(Athens Nat. Museum. Case 47, No. 4573. Hall, *B.S.A.* VIII. p. 188, fig. 30.)

AMENHOTEP II, XVIIIth DYNASTY

86. *Fragments of Faience Plaque.*

Found in house on Acropolis, north-east of Lion Gate.

(1) Se-Ra-Am... (Son of the Sun Am...).
(2) Ta-Ankh...Neb Maat (one of these groups must be upside down), Amenhotep III, 1412–1376 B.C.

There are traces of green glaze. Found with two fibulae.

(*Ibid.* Case 63, No. 2566. Tsountas, *Eph. Arch.* 1891, p. 18, Pl. III; Sewell, *P.S.B.A.* 1904, p. 258.)

AMENHOTEP III, XVIIIth DYNASTY

87. *Fragments of Faience Plaque.*

Found in same house as preceding.

(1) Neter Nefer (good god).
(2) Neter... (god...).
(3) Horizontal line with verticals.

Dull creamy buff ground. Sepia inscription.

Context: L.H. III pottery.

(*Ibid.* Case 59, Nos. 2718–2719. Tsountas, *Eph. Arch.* 1891, Pl. III; Sewell, *P.S.B.A.* 1904, p. 258.)

XVIIIth DYNASTY

*88. *White Paste Scarab.*

Found in ruins of a house south-west of Acropolis, in the rubble. Name of Tiyi, Queen of Amenhotep III (1412–1376 B.C.). (Plate IV.)

Context: bronze rosettes, ivory plaques and great ivory wing (all illustrated on the same plate), L.H. III pottery.

(*Ibid.* Case 63, No. 2530. Tsountas, *Eph. Arch.* 1887, p. 169, Pl. XIII.)

AMENHOTEP III, XVIIIth DYNASTY

GRAVE CIRCLE

89. *Faience Vase.*

Found in Shaft-grave II. Height about 20 cms. With knobs. Restored.

Context: bronze sword, gold cup, M.H. matt painted and L.H. I vases.

(*Ibid.* Case 18, No. 223. Sellers' Schuchardt's *Schliemann*, p. 213.)

XVIIIth DYNASTY

55

*90. *Fragment of Faience Vessel.*

Found in Shaft-grave III. Height about 6 cms. Two men's heads. Warriors of Shairdana type. Banded, horned helmet. Top of great shields. Dr Hall is unconvinced of the Egyptian origin of this object. But I have dared to include it since it has no parallel from Aegean sources. (Cf., with illustration here given, Hall, *Civilization of Greece in the Bronze Age*, p. 137, and the pictures of Shairdana given in that chapter.) (Plate IV.)

Context: gold jewellery and ornaments, seal-stones, etc. Early L.H. I pottery.

(Athens Nat. Museum. Case 14, No. 123. Sellers' Schuchardt's *Schliemann*, p. 208, fig. 198.)

XVIIIth or EARLY XIXth DYNASTY

CHAMBER-TOMBS

91. *Blue Faience Vase.*

Found in Tomb 49. No handles. Design of lotus leaves in light and dark blue alternating, picked out in white filled incisions. (For shape cf. Garstang, *El Amrah*, Pl. XIX, Tomb E 178.)

Cartouche ...menhotep hiq Uast (Amenhotep, Prince of Thebes).

Context: broken ivory cylinder, pottery not given.

(*Ibid.* Case 65, No. 2491. Tsountas, *Eph. Arch.* 1888, p. 156, figs. 10, 10 a.)

AMENHOTEP III, XVIIIth DYNASTY

92–94. *Three Pointed Clay Amphorae.*

Found in unknown chamber-tomb. 56 cms. high. One incised with signs on the handles. (Cf. Peet and Woolley, *City of Akhenaten*, Pl. LII. No. XLIII/260.)

(*Ibid.* Below Cases 59, 60, Nos. 4695, 2924–2925. Tsountas, Μυκῆναι, pp. 213, 214, figs. 1 and 2.)

XVIIIth DYNASTY

*95. *Scarab.*

Found in Tomb 526. White glass paste. Traces of green glaze. Design, "Ankh-Hor-Sa, a foreigner". (Cf. Newberry, *Catalogue of Scarabs in the Cairo Museum*, Pl. VIII. No. 36,786.) (Plate IV.)

XVIIIth DYNASTY

*96. *Scarab.*

From the same tomb. White glass paste. Traces of green glaze. Design, a goose and other signs. (Plate IV.)

Context: L.H. III pottery, and a local imitation in steatite of the above scarabs with four-legged beast and a square within a border.

(*Ibid.* Case 53, unnumbered. *C.A.H.* Illustrations, I. p. 166.)

XVIIIth DYNASTY

MYCENAE

97. *Fragments of Hornblende Porphyry Bowl.*

Found in Tomb 518. 5·5 × 5·3 cms. Typical Old Kingdom work. (Cf. No. 25 from Knossos.)

Context: L.H. III beads, obsidian arrow head, L.H. I–II pottery (some early L.H. III).

(Athens Nat. Museum. Case 53, unnumbered. Evans, *P. of M.* II. i. p. 31, footnote.)

Ist—IInd DYNASTIES

98. *Alabaster Vase.*

Found in Tomb 102 (next to Tomb 505 on road to citadel).[1] Globular body, cylindrical neck, flat handle prolonged with grooved collar round neck below lip. A type derived from Syria but common under Thothmes III or Amenhotep II. (Cf. MacIver and Mace, *El Amrah*, Pl. L. Tomb D. 11.)

Context: another vase of Egyptian alabaster but Minoan work, L.M. II Palace style vase, L.H. II pottery, gold ornaments, steatite lampstands.

(*Ibid.* Case 61, No. 6252. *J.H.S.* XXIV. p. 324, Pl. XIV *e*.)

MID-XVIIIth DYNASTY

THOLOI

99. *Four Fragments of Alabaster Vase.*

Found in deposit earth obstructing doorway of "Treasury of Atreus", in Stamatakis' excavations. Wide flat lip. (Cf. Isopata, Nos. 35, 36, etc.)

Context: M.H., L.H. II and L.H. III sherds.

(*Ibid.* Inventory, No. 95. *B.S.A.* XXV. p. 356.)

XVIIIth DYNASTY

100. *Two Fragments of Alabaster Vase.*

Found in "Tomb of Clytaemnestra" in 1913. Same type of vase as preceding. From the unstratified earth obstructing the doorway and dromos.

Context: one M.H., many L.H. I, II, III sherds.

(*Ibid.* Unidentified. *B.S.A.* XXV. p. 367.)

XVIIIth DYNASTY

PROVENANCE UNKNOWN

101. *Baggy Vase of Banded Alabaster.* About 35 cms. high. (Cf. Isopata, Nos. 35, 36.)

(*Ibid.* Case 61, unnumbered.)

XVIIIth DYNASTY

102. *Alabaster Amphora.*

27 cms. high. Two handles join the neck.

(*Ibid.* Case 61, No. 3225.)

XVIIIth DYNASTY

[1] Wrongly stated by Bosanquet (*J.H.S.* XXIV. *loc. cit.*) to be from a tomb between "Atreus" and "Clytaemnestra", and by Hall (*Civilization of Greece in the Bronze Age*, p. 149) to be from the "Tomb of Aegisthus".

XX. ARGIVE HERAEUM

The Argive Heraeum, situated about three miles from Mycenae on the old Mycenaean road to Nauplia, was, according to tradition, the site of the temple where the Achaeans swore allegiance to Agamemnon before the expedition to Troy. Be that as it may, the site has a long history, dating from Middle Helladic to Roman times. There are Late Helladic chamber-tombs there. There is a great Royal Tholos (Late Helladic II, Wace's second group). There are temples and colonnades of all dates from the seventh century onwards.

It was the sanctuary in Hellenic times of the whole Argolid, and it was naturally here that the sailors of Pheidon and the merchant princes of Argos dedicated the little magic symbols and amulets that they brought from their wanderings.

Many, perhaps most, of the scarabs and figures are from Naucratis. The typically Hellenic-Egyptian "Flute Player" type shows this. But no doubt some came from farther up the Nile, particularly No. 114, which from its careful work may well be a survival from the days of Thothmes III. For the rest they date from the XXVIth Dynasty. Some are good copies of earlier work but spoiled by ignorance of the hieroglyphics proper to the period which they imitate.

They are found chiefly below the second temple, in association with Orientalizing pottery and terracottas. Nothing was found below the black layer of the old temple, and they can safely be dated to the first half of the sixth or last half of the seventh century.

ARGIVE HERAEUM

THOLOS TOMB

03. *Fragment of Bowl.* Found in the Tholos Tomb. Blue glazed faience. Interior decorated with lotus buds in black. (Cf. Hatshepsut and Thothmes III at Der el Baḥri.)

(Athens Nat. Museum. Case 76, No. 3335. *B.S.A.* xxv. p. 336, fig. 68 *g*.)
XVIIIth DYNASTY

104. *Two Fitting Fragments of Alabaster Vase.* Also from Tholos. Wide flat lip. (Cf. Isopata, Nos. 35, 36.)

Context: necklace, studs, gold foil, gold beads, boars' tusks for helmet, green steatite lamps, pottery—mostly L.H. II, of poor work.

(*Ibid.* Case 76, No. 3336. *B.S.A.* xxv. p. 336.)
XVIIIth DYNASTY

CHAMBER-TOMB

105. *Scarab.* Found in Chamber-tomb 14. White glass paste. "The good god Amen" (?).

Context: Mycenaean daggers. L.H. I pottery.

(*Ibid.* Room 29, Case 214, unnumbered. *A.J.A.* 1925, p. 427.)
EARLY XVIIIth DYNASTY

BELOW SANCTUARY, SECOND TEMPLE

106. *Scarab 5.* Frit. Glaze gone. Amen-Ra (Amen-Ra).

107. *Scarab 6.* Blue glazed frit. Same inscription as above. Careful work.

108. *Scarab 7.* Blue glazed frit. Amen-Ra-Neb-Maat (Amen-Ra, Lord of Truth). Careless. Confused reading of name of Amen-hotep III.

109. *Scarab 8.* Traces of blue glaze. Similar to above.

110. *Scarab 9.* Blue glazed. Ankh Maat (Maat liveth).

111. *Scarab 10.* Glaze disappeared. Ra-Neb-Maat (Ra, Lord of Truth) and uraeus. Cf. No. 108 above.

112. *Scarab 12.* Frit. No traces of glaze. Ra-Nefer-Neb-Maat (Beautiful is Ra, Lord of Truth).

113. *Scarab 17.* Deep yellow glazed steatite. Men-kheper-Ra (Thothmes III). Red crown of the north and the royal mace.
XXVIth DYNASTY

114. *Scarab 18.* Faience. Glaze gone. Nesut-biti (King of Upper and Lower Egypt). Cartouche below. Men-kheper-Ra (Thothmes III, 1501–1447 B.C.) between uraei.
THOTHMES III, XVIIIth DYNASTY

59

115. *Scarab* 19.	Soft paste. Men-kheper-Ra (?). Much worn.
116. *Scarab* 20.	Deep blue frit. Glaze gone. Sun's disk. Ship of Ra. Hawk.
117. *Scarab* 22.	Blue glazed frit. Sphinx. Sun's disk. Feather.
118. *Scarab* 23.	Frit. Glaze gone. Ship of Ra. Disk. Uraeus.
119. *Scarab* 24.	Blue glazed frit. Hiq (Prince). Uraeus and "di" (= give).
120. *Scarab* 26.	Yellow glazed frit. Disk. Ra seated.
121. *Scarab* 27.	Frit. Glaze gone. King in crown of south holding sceptre and uraeus.
122. *Scarab* 28.	Frit. Glaze gone. Jackal.
123. *Scarab* 29.	Blue glazed frit. Menthu, hawk-headed, plumed, holding "Uast" (Theban) sceptre, before seated Osiris.
124. *Scarab* 30.	Frit. Glaze gone. Ankh. Uraei intertwined.
125. *Scarab* 31.	Frit. Glaze gone. Griffin.
126. *Scarab* 32.	Pale blue-grey pottery. Two ibexes running.
127. *Scarab* 33.	Pale blue glazed pottery. Ibex pursued by hound.
128. *Scarab* 34.	Dark brown faience. Duck rising from marsh and sedge.
129. *Scarab* 35.	Blue glazed frit. Sun's disk. Sphinx. Hawk and papyrus.
130, 131. *Scarabs* 36, 37.	Frit so worn as to be undecipherable.
132. *Scarab* 38.	Frit. Winged uraeus protecting sun's disk.
133. *Scarab* 39.	Frit. Greenish blue glaze. Seated divinity between winged uraei.
134. *Amulet* 42.	Papyrus capital in blue faience.
135. *Amulet* 43.	"Ab", the heart amulet. Crystal.
136. *Amulet* 44.	"Ab", the heart amulet. In blue faience.
137. *Human Head in Massive Wig* 45.	Broken off male figure. Blue faience.
138. *Bes* 47.	Statuette in blue glazed faience. Feather crown broken off.
139. *Cat* 48.	Seated. White glazed faience.
140. *Figure* 49.	Ptah from Ptah-Sokar-Asar group. Blue glazed faience.
141. *Hare* 54.	Crouching. Blue glazed faience.
142. *Fragment* 55.	Indeterminate in form. Blue glazed faience.
143. *Two Fragments of Vase* 56 *and* 57.	In blue glazed faience. Double band moulded in relief, ribs and rosettes.
144. *Whorl* 58.	Daisy rosette on either side. Blue glazed faience.

145. *Whorl* 59.

Sharply pointed petal design on either side. Blue glazed faience.

146. *Fragment of Group* 60.

Originally two figures, man and wife, in heavy wigs, side by side. In blue glazed faience. Wigs coloured black.

147. *Kneeling Figure* 61.

Base and lower part only. In blue glazed faience.

All from American excavations, 1892–1895. Numbers beside objects refer to cataloguing in Waldstein's *Heraeum*. Missing numbers occupied by "Flute Players".

Context: Orientalizing vases and terracottas.

(Athens Nat. Museum. Room 29, Case 182. Waldstein, *Argive Heraeum*, p. 370, Pl. CXLIII.)

XXVIth DYNASTY (except No. 114)

XXI. DENDRA

The site lies under the old hill fort of Midea north of Tiryns. In 1926–1927 the Swedes discovered a great royal tholos and a number of chamber-tombs. Though the chief interest of the site is undoubtedly in the rich treasures of the tholos, a further proof of the intercourse between Egypt and the Mainland of Greece has appeared in the chamber-tombs.

DENDRA

148. *Alabaster Vase.*

Found in Chamber-tomb 2 inside the doorway. Baggy type (compared by the excavator to those from Isopata).

Context: three Cretan steatite lamps and four alabaster vases, L.H. III pottery.

(Not displayed in Museum. Persson, *Kungagraven i Dendra*, p. 150.)

XVIIIth DYNASTY

XXII. ASINE

Asine on the gulf of Tolon, about six miles south of Nauplia, is mentioned in Homer. The remains consist of a fort on the promontory running out to sea and a large number of Late Helladic and Geometric tombs on the hill behind.

The fort commands a magnificent view and would be a very suitable watch-tower against hostile ships approaching from the south and attempting to beach out of sight of Nauplia, thus enabling the men to march straight into the heart of the Argolid.

In Mycenaean times it was a fort pure and simple. No surrounding houses of that period have been discovered.

The stone bowl which Dr Persson discovered here he believes to have been brought from Crete where it had been an heirloom. It was again an heirloom on the Mainland and thus managed to pass the two and a half thousand years of its existence above ground. I should prefer to believe that the owner with whom it was buried had carried on a little tomb-robbing either when raiding Egypt or when serving Pharaoh as a mercenary.

ASINE

149. *Bowl.*

Found in Tomb 2. Hornblende porphyry. 12 cms. high. 12 cms. across mouth. Lip stands up but is not undercut. Perforated roll handles. (Cf. Knossos, No. 26.)

(Nauplia Museum. Case 13, No. 1307.)

Ist—IInd DYNASTIES

150. *Ivory Head of a Duck.*

From the same tomb. End of spoon, or top of kohl pot or ointment vase.

Context: Palace style vase. Rest of pottery chiefly L.H. III. Fluted stone vase, gold necklets and beads.

(*Ibid.* Case 12, unnumbered. Persson, *Asine*, 1922, Pl. XXXIX.)

XVIIIth DYNASTY

XXIII. CALAURIA

The ruins of Calauria lie at the north-eastern corner of the Island of Poros. They are very scanty and consist mainly of a few stoae, a propylaeum, and a very ancient temple of Poseidon.

Calauria is known as the religious centre of a sacred league of maritime states of the eastern coast of Greece. It goes back to pre-Dorian—perhaps even to pre-Achaean— days (*C.A.H.* III. p. 650). The members were Epidaurus, Aegina, Athens, Boeotian Orchomenos (through her subject-port Anthedon), Hermione, Prasiae (on the coast of the Peloponnese), and Nauplia. After the Dorian conquest Argos replaces Nauplia, and Sparta Prasiae.

151. *Carnelian Scaraboid.* Found in inner hall of the old temple. Pharaoh charging in his chariot. The back worked into the form of a hippopotamus (cf. scaraboid, said to be from Calauria, seen in Athens in hands of a dealer, eye of Horus, back worked into hippopotamus also). (Cf. *B.S.A.* xiii. p. 88 ff.; Newberry, *Scarabs*, p. 85; and Hall, *Catalogue of Scarabs in the British Museum*, No. 1514.)

Context: found immediately above L.H. deposit.

(I am unable to discover where this scarab now is. *Ath. Mitt.* 1895, pp. 300–302, fig. 20.)

EARLY XVIIIth DYNASTY

CORINTHIA

XXIV. CORINTH

XXIV. CORINTH

Considering the close connection which history shows between Corinth and Egypt in the seventh century, when tyrants of Corinth could give their sons Egyptian names—Psammetichus, Psammis—and enter into alliance on almost equal terms, it is surprising that only one piece of Egyptian work has ever come from there, and even that is uncertain, for it was bought in Athens. Excavation, however, has only just begun to reach the seventh-century stratum, and it may confidently be prophesied that many more pieces of concrete evidence will turn up.

CORINTH

152. *Vase.*

White clay. Blue glaze. 6·5 cms. high. In shape of head of warrior. Helmet covers the cheeks. Yellow is used for details and black for eyes. On it is the cartouche of King Uah-ab-Ra, Psamtek I (663–609 B.C.). This name might be that of King Haa-ab-Ra, Uah-ab-Ra (Apries 589–565 B.C.), and is usually so taken. As, however, the throne name is more usually used alone I have attributed this to Psamtek.

No context, as the vase was bought in Athens.

(Louvre. Room A, No. 102. *C.A.H.* Illustrations, I. p. 298. Heuzey, *Cat. Fig. Ant. du Louvre*, Pl. III. No. 2.)

PSAMTEK I, XXVIth DYNASTY

ATTICA

XXV. MENIDI (ACHARNAE)

Menidi is the ancient Acharnae about seven miles north of Athens. The tholos tomb in which the following were discovered is built of rough limestone slabs, and appears to be later, if anything, than all the Mycenaean examples.

MENIDI (ACHARNAE)

153–156. *Four Pointed Amphorae.*

Found in tholos. 35 cms. high. Pale non-Mycenaean clay. Undecipherable marks incised on handles, probably after clay was hard, are records of quantity, value or ownership. (Cf. Peet and Woolley, *City of Akhenaten*, Pl. LII. No. XLIII/67.)

Context: seals, beads, ivory and bone ornaments, Late L.H. III and Geometric pottery in dromos.

(Athens Nat. Museum. Mycenaean Room, below Cases 83–86, Nos. 2014–2017. *J.H.S.* XXIV. p. 329. Lolling, *Kuppelgrab*, Pl. IX. Nos. 1–4.)

XVIIIth DYNASTY

XXVI. ATHENS

The only Egyptian objects found in Athens antedate by far our knowledge of any historic connections. There is no trace of anything which could be dated to the great period of Athenian trade. As in the case of Thebes, it looks as if these three small works must be the "souvenirs" of some returned adventurer of the Late Geometric Period rather than the evidence of peaceful trade.

157, 158. *Two Lions.*

Found in a tomb in the Dipylon Cemetery below K. Sapount-zakis' house. 6 cms. long. Faience. Traces of blue glaze. Couchant. Inscriptions on base:

(1) Illegible.

(2) ...Ra Aahmes.

Context: Geometric vases, Nos. 770–775, in the same case.

(Athens Nat. Museum. Vase Room 1, Case 4, Nos. 780, 781. *B.C.H.* 1893, p. 189.)

XXIInd—XXVIth DYNASTIES

*159. *Horus (Harpocrates).*

Bronze statuette found on the Acropolis. 11·2 cms. high. Right hand and left forearm missing, also side lock and throne. Seated in usual attitude, finger to lips. Uraeus on brow. (Plate IV.)

Context: unknown.

(*Ibid.* Bronze Room, Case 194, No. 6591. *J.H.S.* XIII. p. 240. De Ridder, *Bronzes de l'Acropole*, p. 280.)

XXVIth DYNASTY

XXVII. ELEUSIS

The finds at Eleusis show that the town was in fairly close communication with Egypt in the dark ages of the twelfth and seventh centuries. Eleusis at that time was of course not dependent upon Athens. She was a free city, and her citizens may well have gone raiding or trading to the south.

TOMB OF ISIS

160. *Figure of Isis.*   Faience. Wearing the horned moon. 5·4 cms. high.

XXth—XXIInd DYNASTIES

161. *Scarab.*   Faience. Men-kheper-Ra, son of Pinezem I, the priest-king, *c.* 1050 B.C. Below, a vase between uraei. (Cf. Hall, *Catalogue of Scarabs in the British Museum*, No. 2382.)

MEN-KHEPER-RA, XXIst DYNASTY

162. *Scarab.*   Faience. Amen-Ra Neb (Taui?) (Amen-Ra the Lord) (of the two Lands (?)).

XXth—XXIInd DYNASTIES

163. *Scarab.*   Faience:

Context: gold pectoral of Egyptian influence and Late Geometric ware.

XXth—XXIInd DYNASTIES

TOMB A

164. *Scarab.*   Green faience. Vulture with outspread wings standing on beetle between birds.

Context: gold pectoral similar to preceding and Late Geometric ware.

XXth—XXIInd DYNASTIES

TELESTERION or OUTSIDE

165. *Scarab in Green Faience.*   Men-(kheper)-Ra between reed sign (Nesut = Royal symbol of the North) and vase (Hes), or possibly "Praised is Amen-Ra, Lord and King".

166. *Scarab.*   Reddish brown frit. Thoth holding sceptre. Hawk of Horus.

167. *Scarab.*   Glaze gone. "Psamtek"—a common name at this period.

168. *Scarab.*   Glaze gone. Squatting lion (?), sun over his back, in front a rectangular sign.

169. *Scarab.*   Traces of blue glaze. Goose facing right.

170. *Scarab.*   Brown frit. Winged griffin facing right.

171. *Scarab.*   Glaze gone. Reed and feather.

172. *Scarab.*   Traces of blue glaze. Men-(kheper)-Ra. Ichneumon and snake below.

173. *Scarab.*   Green glaze, nearly gone. Amen-Ra and looped sign.

ELEUSIS

174. *Scarab.* Green glaze. Two indecipherable signs:

175. *Fragment in Green Glaze.* Possibly the beginning of the name of Amen.

All found in and around oldest building on site of Telesterion, i.e. dating from somewhere in the first half of the seventh century.

(All in Store Room of Eleusis Museum. *Eph. Arch.* 1898, pp. 107, 120, Pl. VI.)

XXVIth DYNASTY

XXVIII. SUNIUM

Sunium—the sanctuary of the seafarers of Athens—the site of the temple of Poseidon, though having no separate existence apart from Athens and therefore to be reckoned as Athens, was the natural place of dedication for the early merchant adventurers. It is here rather than at Eleusis that we must look for traces of intercourse between Athens and Egypt—live intercourse that is—for the dedications and deposits here are the honest treasures and "lucks" of Attic sailors brought from a far country, not amulets bought to place in a tomb with some hope of mysterious benefits for the dead, but "curios" dedicated in thankfulness to Poseidon by the living.

They date chiefly from the middle of the seventh century, i.e. the early XXVIth Dynasty, and are all from the Precinct of Poseidon, in a deposit in the Eastern Angle of the Temenos. The rest of the objects found in this deposit, as will be seen below, cannot be dated much before the middle of the sixth century.

176. *Scarab of Green Paste.*	Small. Maat-Ra (The Sun's Truth).
177. *Scarab of Green Paste.*	Larger. Se-Ra-Ankh (The Son of the Sun liveth).
*178. *Scarab of Green Paste.*	Larger still. Two hawks on the ship of Ra. (Plate IV.)
*179. *Scarab of Green Paste.*	Small. Ankh Horu (Horus is living). The hawk of Horus has the double crown. (Plate IV.)
180. *Scarab of Green Paste.*	Smaller. A beetle. Kheper.
*181. *Scarab of Green Paste.*	Very small. Amen-Ra. (Plate IV.)
*182. *Circular Seal.*	Lion and sun. (Plate IV.)
*183. *Figure.*	Green glazed figurine. Upper half only. Magic implements at side (cf. statue of Khaemuast in B.M.). Elaborate collar. Curious headdress. Indecipherable inscription down back. (Plate IV.)
*184. *Figure of Ptah.*	Green glazed figurine. Head gone. Indecipherable inscription on back. (Plate IV.)
*185. *Figure of Crouching Lion.*	Amulet. Yellowish glaze. Hole for attachment gone. (Plate IV.)
186. *Standing Figure.*	Female. Lower half only. Broken inscription on back.
187. *Figure of Osiris.*	Small. Headless. Faience.
188. *Standing Figure.*	Very rough. Faience. With large wig. Standing against square column.
189. *Hawk.*	Yellow glaze. 6 cms. high. To be attached as amulet.
190, 191. *Two Hawks.*	Greenish glaze. 3 cms. high. Amulets. (Athens Nat. Museum. Case 111, Box No. 14,928.)
192. *Circular Seal.*	Uraeus and feather.
193. *Circular Seal.*	Man holding sceptre. Very rough.
194, 195. *Circular Seals.*	Two seals with ibex and sun.
196–198. *Circular Seals.*	Three seals with lion and sun.
199. *Scarab.*	Green paste. Indecipherable.
200. *Scarab.*	Small. Green glaze. Two wavy horizontal signs and eagle to the right. Very worn—possibly for Sebek-hotep. (Cf. Hall, *Catalogue of Scarabs in the British Museum*, No. 190.)
201. *Scarab.*	Reddish frit. Ra. Thoth.
202. *Scarab.*	Glaze gone. Bad writing. Possibly a garbled version of "Neb-Maat-Ra" (Amenhotep III).

203. *Scarab.*	Glaze gone. Clump of lotus.
204. *Scarab.*	Green glaze. Long-tailed beast. Sun over back. Triangular sign in front.
*205. *Scarab.*	Glaze gone. Very careful. Ptah. (Plate IV.)
206. *Scarab.*	Glaze gone. Two hawks confront above. Two gods below.
207. *Scarab.*	Glaze gone. Small. Ankh between uraei.
208. *Scarab.*	Brown paste. Amen-Ra Ded (Amen-Ra is stable).
209. *Scarab.*	Brown paste. Lion and sun.
210. *Scarab.*	Brown paste. Long-tailed winged beast with sun on head.
211. *Scarab.*	Brown paste. Bes.
212. *Scarab.*	Brown paste. Lion. Sun over back. Feather in front.
*213. *Scarab.*	Brown paste. Se-Ra (Son of the Sun) and indistinct sign. (Plate IV.)
214. *Scarab.*	Brown paste. Lion, sun over back. Feather in front.
215. *Scarab.*	White paste. Very small and delicate. Amen-Ra.
216, 217. *Scarabs.*	Indecipherable, nearly rotted.
218. *Scarab.*	Brown paste. Long-tailed winged beast with disk on head.
*219. *Scarab.*	Paste. Two uraei emerging from side of disk, one from top. (Plate IV.)
*220. *Scarab.*	Paste. Lion and sun. Triangle in front. (Plate IV.)
221. *Scarab.*	Dark green glaze. Goddess with outspread wings.
222. *Scarab.*	Brown paste. Lion and sun.
223. *Lozenge-shaped Object.*	Uraeus and sun disk. Men-kheper-Ra (?).
224. *Lozenge-shaped Object.*	Lion and sun.
225. *Scarab.*	Glaze gone. Nesut biti (King of Upper and Lower Egypt). Together with obvious imitation scarabs in dark blue pottery. Most are inscribed with a goddess holding a sceptre and a bird. Some with Thoth (?) between two figures. Very rude.

Context: bronze figure of hoplite, bronze animal, spear heads, rings, etc., clay plaques with figure of woman, Herakles and lion, etc. Style of mid-sixth century. Corinthian Bombyllios.

(Athens Nat. Museum. Case 111, Box No. 14,937. *Eph. Arch.* 1917, p. 196.)

XXVIth DYNASTY

BOEOTIA

XXIX. THEBES

XXIX. THEBES

There is no historical record of any traffic between Thebes and Egypt. Indeed there is no place in which it would be more unlikely to find any trace of such. This one object is obviously a "souvenir" of some wandering adventurer of the Geometric Period.

THEBES

*226. *Scarab.*

Steatite. Ankh, in front of winged sphinx wearing the double crown. From a tomb. (Plate III.)

Context: Geometric pottery.

(British Museum. 1st Vase Room, Case F, unnumbered. Hall, *Ancient History of Near East*, p. 521, footnote.)

XIXth DYNASTY

THESSALY

XXX. VELESTINO (PHERAE)

XXX. VELESTINO (PHERAE)

Pherae, always one of the chief towns of Thessaly, lies some way inland to the west of the northern point of the Pagasaean Gulf. As is the case with the rest of early Thessaly, we know little or nothing of its early history until the perfection of the League soon before 700 B.C.; but it must have been the centre of a landed aristocracy.

Since there were no trading interests it is surprising that any foreign object has found its way thither; it is probably a "souvenir" brought back by some Thessalian adventurer of the Geometric Age. More we cannot say until the publication of other finds takes place, among which are said to be scarabs and works in faience.

VELESTINO (PHERAE)

*227. Bronze Situla.

Height 12 cms. One handle broken. Four zones of decoration in relief:

(1) Below the moulded lip, capering animals.

(2) Wide middle band. Figures of gods. Neith, Amen, Ptah, Horus, Isis, Nepthys, Min, and a man behind a table of offerings advances to meet them.

(3) Narrow band below. Anubis, Taurt, Hekt. Winged sphinx, other bestial gods.

(4) Rayed base.

(Cf. Petrie, *Dendereh*, Pl. XXIV. No. 12.) (Plate III.)

Context: probably Geometric bronze birds, etc.

(Fitzwilliam Museum, Cambridge. Case of bronzes.)

XXIInd—XXVIth DYNASTIES

ISLANDS

XXXI. AEGINA

The Aeginetans were the most powerful trading people of Greece in archaic times. They had a concession at Naucratis and built themselves a precinct there under the patronage of Pharaoh Aahmes II, 570–526 B.C. The sea-power of Aegina was no doubt fostered by King Pheidon of Argos who seems to have dominated most of the Saronic Gulf in the early seventh century. He probably struck the first coins ever minted on the Mainland in this island, and it was this legacy of his which was their great power in later times.

The two sites where Egyptian objects have been found are the two precincts: that of Aphrodite on the west coast by Aegina Town, and that of Aphaia in the pine woods overlooking the eastern shore. That the majority of these objects come from Naucratis is made almost certain by the presence of many faience figures of Flute-Players, a common combination at Naucratis of an Egyptian material and a Hellenic subject.

It is not my intention here to do anything but state the facts, but there is one point which is well worth investigation. Aegina is Peloponnesian, probably by race, certainly by sympathy; she always ranks herself with the Peloponnese whether in weight, standards or weapons. How is it that she has not more in common with the Peloponnesian school of art? How is it that whereas the Argive school and the rest of the early fifth-century Peloponnesians delight in heavy, almost over-muscled, figures, Aegina produces these marvels of slimness and lightness? Is it possible that it is due to the influence of the Saite art of the previous century? The Saites had gone back to the Pyramid Age for their models. They loved the slim, high-shouldered, rather dry figure, very light on its feet. Is it possible that it is the Greek passion for motion, coupled with the Saite love for slimness, that has produced these masterpieces?

AEGINA

From early building period, consisting of Propylaeum and early Altar. The following are in the Aegina Museum. First room to right, right-hand case at the end.

228.	*Large Scarab.*	Greenish paste. Very indistinct, figure seated on animal. Another figure behind.
229.	*Large Scarab.*	Brown paste. Winged double-crowned figure. Above wings uraei emerge from sun's disk; below wings Thoth and Sekhet.
230.	*Scarab.*	White paste. "Hor-Sa-Neb".
231.	*Scarab.*	White paste. Uraeus confronts figure of Maat (Goddess of Truth).
232.	*Scarab.*	White paste. (Men)-kheper-Ra, Neb and a feather of Maat to fill in space.
233.	*Scarab.*	White paste. ...Nefer ...User? Very badly written and garbled.
234.	*Scarab.*	Greyish paste. "Iqer" (excellent)....Broken.
235.	*Scarab.*	Bluish grey paste. Ichneumon and lotus. (Aegina Museum. Nos. 210, 216, 228.)
236.	*Figurine of Ram.*	Light green glaze. (*Ibid.* No. 194.)
237.	*Base and Feet of Ibis.*	Light green glaze. (*Ibid.* No. 197.)
238.	*Amulet in Form of Table of Offerings.*	Bluish glaze. Base for hawk on top. One end inscribed "The beautiful Bull of Truth". (*Ibid.* No. 275.)
239.	*Ointment Vase.*	6·5 cms. high. Baggy alabaster. Knobs below lips for holding. (*Ibid.* No. 430.)
240.	*Hawk.*	1 cm. high. Green glaze. Headless. (*Ibid.* No. 417.)
241.	*Hawk.*	3 cms. high. Green glaze. (*Ibid.* No. 196.)
242.	*Lion.*	3 cms. long. Crouching. Green glaze. (*Ibid.* No. 193.)
243.	*Squat Bowl.*	Neck and handle only. Fine blue glaze. Flat lip which handle joins. (*Ibid.* No. 199.)
244–248.	*Five Spindle Whorls.*	Blue paste. Daisy pattern on top. (*Ibid.* Unnumbered.)

XXVIth DYNASTY

AEGINA

Of the following I was unable to find any trace in the Museums. The numbers below refer to Furtwängler's second volume, pp. 387–388.

249. *Standing Figure.*	3·5 cms. high. Faience. Torso only. Arms to sides. (No. 12.)	
250. *Standing Figure.*	5 cms. high. Faience. Lower part only. Long kilt. (No. 13.)	
251. *Kneeling Woman.*	Faience. Lower part only. (No. 18.)	
252. *Crouching Man.*	Headless. Light blue glaze. (No. 20.)	
253. *Squatting Ape.*	Lower part only. Faience. (No. 25.)	
254. *Large Scarab.*	Fragment only. Faience. (No. 27.)	
255. *Standing Figure.*	1·8 cms. high. Lower half only. Harpocrates (?). White glaze. (No. 47.)	

Context: uncertain, owing to foundations of later buildings causing disturbed stratification.

XXVIth DYNASTY

TEMPLE OF APHRODITE

The following are in the same room of the Aegina Museum as the first group, but in the left-hand case at the end.

256. *Scarab.*	White paste. Broken. Sekhmet holding tall lotus sceptre. A broken cartouche in front. (Aegina Museum. No. 905.)
257. *Scarab.*	White paste. Very indistinct. A bird and some symbol. (*Ibid.* Unnumbered.)
258–260. *Three Spindle Whorls.*	Blue glaze. Daisy pattern in black. (*Ibid.* Unnumbered.)
261. *Figure of Bes.*	5 cms. high. White paste. Traces of red paint behind. Legs broken. (*Ibid.* No. 906.)
262. *Standing Male Figure.*	3·4 cms. high. White paste. Legs only. (*Ibid.* No. 907.)
263. *Lotus-Capital Amulet.*	Top only. Traces of green glaze. (*Ibid.* No. 908.)

97

264. *Large Spindle Whorl.*	Blue glaze. Daisy pattern in black. (*Ibid.* No. 909.)	
265, 266. *Fragments of Two Squat Bowls.*	Necks only (cf. No. 243 above). Blue glaze. (*Ibid.* No. 1411.)	
267. *Amen.*	Figure of god, bearded. Flat cap. Greenish glaze. To be suspended as amulet. (*Ibid.* No. 900.)	
268. *Base.*	White paste. Two feet, very small. (*Ibid.* Unnumbered.)	
269. *Fragment of Ichneumon* (?).	Brownish paste. (*Ibid.* Unnumbered.)	

XXVIth DYNASTY

The following is in the Athens National Museum, Vase Room I, Case 9, No. 10,826.

270. *Crouching Lion.* Greenish glaze. 5·6 cms. long. Found under coping of Eastern Terrace of Temple of Aphrodite.
(Furtwängler, p. 387, No. 21.)

Context: again uncertain owing to the presence of very old houses of the Middle Helladic Period into which the foundations have cut.

XXVIth DYNASTY

The following are in the Athens National Museum, in the same tray as above. They are all illustrated in the final plate of Waldstein's *Argive Heraeum*, but unfortunately there is no indication as to which temple they came from.

271. *Head of Bes.*	3 cms. high. Faience. Feather crown. Large ears.
272. *Faience Fragment.*	Curved as if part of a pectoral. Blue in colour. Incised duck among reeds.
273. *Lid of Kohl Pot.*	Blue glazed faience. Centre in relief, represents daisy.
274. *Seated Cat.*	5·3 cms. high. Blue green, black and dark green glaze.
275. *Scarab on Bronze Ring.*	Much decayed. Glaze gone. Illegible.
276. *Scarab.*	Two uraei back to back.
277. *Scarab.*	Green glaze. Ra seated with hawk's head and disk. Plume of Maat in front.
278. *Scarab.*	Uraeus and two feathers. Glaze gone.
279. *Scarab.*	Goddess with spread wings, uraeus and disk.
280–283. *Four Scarabs.*	Illegible. Glaze gone.
284–286. *Three Spindle Whorls.*	Blue glaze. Daisy pattern in black.

XXVIth DYNASTY

XXXII. EUBOEA (CHALCIS)

Chalcis—the great port on the narrow straits of the Euripos, was one of the great Greek trading cities of early Hellenic times. At first, like Eretria, she relied on the local purple fisheries for her wealth, but she soon expanded—chiefly to the north—Chalcidice—and to the western Mediterranean.

At the end of the eighth century Chalcis and Eretria were notable enough to set the Greek world by the ears during their petty squabble of the "Lelantic Plain". But her sea power was over by the beginning of the sixth century. It had passed to Aegina and Corinth.

At no time did Chalcis take any interest in the eastern Mediterranean and she seems to have had no dealings at Naucratis.

The following object is probably from one of the Mycenaean tombs excavated by Papavasileiou in 1902. It is so labelled in the Museum, but is not mentioned in his Οἱ Ἀρχαῖοι Τάφοι τῆς Χαλκίδος.

EUBOEA (CHALCIS)

287. *Alabaster Vase.*   A baggy vase of banded alabaster with two knobs under the lip. 11 cms. high. (Cf. Isopata, Nos. 35, 36.)

No context known.

(Athens Nat. Museum. Terracotta Room 1, Case 173, No. 13,645.)

XVIIIth DYNASTY

XXXIII. CHIOS (PHANA)

Phana lies close to the southern extremity of Chios. Here, in 1913, Kourouniotis excavated the site of the temple of "Apollo in Phanai". The following objects were found in a geometric deposit within the wall of the precinct.

As this is one of the few sites which have been excavated on the island, since the end of Turkish rule made excavation possible, we must wait for further evidence before we can state the duration of the connection between this powerful and rich island and Egypt. That there was such connection we know, not only from this stray piece of evidence but also from the fact that the Chians, together with the Aeginetans, Milesians and Samians, were among the original "claim holders" at Naucratis and shared in the Hellenion (Herodotus, II. 180).

CHIOS (PHANA)

288. *Faience Female Figure.*

Height 7 ins. Glaze gone. Breasts and hair black. Short illegible inscription down back.

(Chios Museum. End central case, unnumbered. *Arch. Delt.* 1915, p. 79, fig. 17.)

XXIInd—XXVIth DYNASTIES

289. *Faience Scarab.*

Pale blue glaze. Two lions confront with heads turned back.

Context for both the above: Geometric pottery, an imitation Phoenician scarab.

(*Ibid.* No. 529. *Arch. Delt.* 1915, p. 79.)

XXIInd—XXVIth DYNASTIES

XXXIV. PAROS (DELION)

The Delion on Paros lies on the west coast north of the modern town of Paroikia, and an hour's walk away. The Sanctuary was dedicated to Apollo, Artemis and Leto. It consisted of a temenos wall, a rock altar and a small temple in antis in the north-west corner.

Paros enjoyed an utterly undistinguished history, and these few objects are the only trace we have of any outside connection at all.

PAROS (DELION)

290. *Spindle Whorl.*

Blue faience. Black daisy pattern.

(Paroikia Museum. Middle room, left-hand case, No. 159.)

291–293. *Three Figures of Bes.*

Blue faience. 4 ins. high.

Context: Orientalizing pottery early terracotta and a few other broken fragments of faience (cf. *Arch. Anz.* 1900, p. 20).

(*Ibid.* Nos. 155, 156, 158.)

XXVIth DYNASTY

XXXV. SAMOS

Although we know from literary sources of the close connection between Samos and Egypt, excavation has brought to light but one Egyptian object—and the context of that has been lost. Samos was one of the first in the field at Naucratis, and a little later her tyrant Polycrates was on terms of personal friendship and alliance with Pharaoh Aahmes II (Amasis). Prior to this there is no evidence for intercourse, Samos was—and until lately almost always has been—part of Asia Minor, and it seems as if her history in the Bronze Age has no more connection with the outer world than as a mere stepping-stone for waves of intruders who have left a trace of their stay in the Early and Middle Helladic pottery.

SAMOS

294. *Bronze Figure of Apis.*
Length 9 cms. Much patinated. Traces of engraved decorations. Horns and disk lost.

This figure has lost its context and indeed all record during its removal to the new Museum.

(Vathy Museum. Case Γ, No. 901.)

XXVIth DYNASTY

XXXVI. THERA

Thera has always played an unimportant part in history. There is no record of her trade with foreign lands. Herodotus (IV. 149) says that the island was colonized by the Spartans under Theras, and certainly the two following objects bear a striking resemblance in style, date and context to those scarabs found in the earliest stratum of the Sanctuary of Orthia at Sparta (q.v.). The tomb they came from is on the hill of Sellada just above the site of the town in the south-east corner of the island.

THERA

From the "Archaic Grave" on Sellada.

295. *White Paste Scarab on Silver Ring.*

Rough inscription "Khonsu in Thebes" (?)

(Thera Museum. Case 8, No. 100. *Thera*, II. p. 298, fig. 488 *g*.)

XXIInd—XXVIth DYNASTIES

296. *White Paste Scarab.*

Larger. Ring broken off. Two rude figures support a cartouche, surmounted by two plumes, containing a garbled version of Men-kheper-Ra or Men-kau-Ra.

Context for both the above: Local Geometric pottery.

(*Ibid.* No. 101. *Thera*, II. p. 298, fig. 488 *h*.)

XXIInd—XXVIth DYNASTIES

XVII. SPARTA (*cont.*)

The following scarabs are of interest as providing two of the earliest objects yet found on the Mainland. It is curious that at Sparta there is to be found such a deposit, covering a period of over a thousand years and proving that the Geometric Spartan was not above buying "genuine antiques" on his travels, for obviously these must have been so acquired. The references are to the full publication of the Sanctuary of Artemis Orthia, Chapter XI, Section 3.

297. *Blue Faience Scarab.*	Glaze gone. Inscribed "Senusert." (Pl. CCV. No. 2.) *XIIth DYNASTY*
298. *Blue Faience Scarab.*	Glaze gone. Design of radiating petals and flowers. (Pl. CCV. No. 10.) *SECOND INTERMEDIATE PERIOD*
299. *Blue Faience Scarab.*	Glaze gone. Figure of Maat. (Pl. CCV. No. 7.) *XVIIIth DYNASTY*
300. *Blue Faience Scarab.*	Glaze gone. Two goats. (Pl. CCV. No. 8.) *XVIIIth DYNASTY*
301. *Blue Faience Scarab.*	Glaze gone. A man and a ram. (Pl. CCV. No. 12.) *XVIIIth DYNASTY*
302. *Blue Faience Scarab.*	Glaze gone. A rough winged figure. Symbols in the field. (Pl. CCV. No. 3.) *XIXth DYNASTY*
303. *Blue Faience Scarab.*	Glaze gone. A calf. (Pl. CCV. No. 1.) *XIXth DYNASTY*
304. *Blue Faience Scarab.*	Glaze gone. A lion (?). Symbols in the field. (Pl. CCV. No. 6.) *XIXth DYNASTY*
305. *Blue Faience Scarab.*	Glaze gone. Rough hieroglyphs. (Pl. CCV. No. 11.) *XXVIth DYNASTY*
306. *Blue Faience Ram.*	3 cms. high. (Pl. CCVI. No. 13.) *XXVIth DYNASTY*
307. *Blue Faience Kohl Pot.*	5 cms. high. Frieze of ducks and lotus flowers. (Pl. CCVI. No. 1.) *XXVIth DYNASTY*

Context of Nos. 297–300 and Nos. 302–304: Geometric pottery; Nos. 301, 305: Geometric and Laconian I pottery; Nos. 306, 307: Laconian I and Orientalizing pottery.

Many other scarabs and fragments of vases.

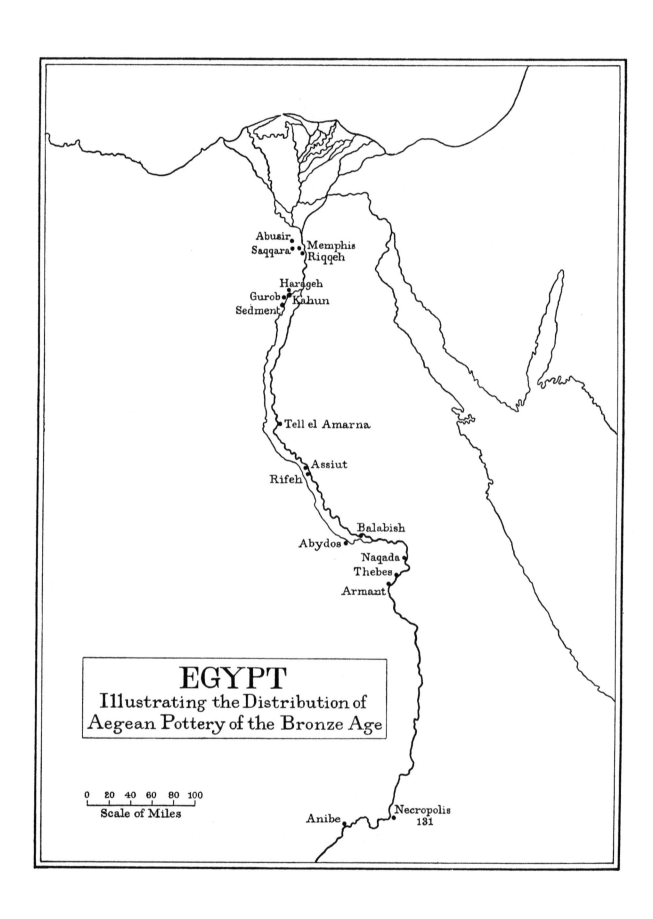

Abusir
Saqqara
Memphis
Riqqeh

Harageh
Gurob
Kahun
Sedment

Tell el Amarna

Assiut
Rifeh

Balabish
Abydos
Naqada
Thebes
Armant

EGYPT
Illustrating the Distribution of
Aegean Pottery of the Bronze Age

0 20 40 60 80 100
Scale of Miles

Anibe
Necropolis
131

NOTE ON AEGEAN POTTERY OF THE BRONZE AGE FOUND IN EGYPT

The following list is almost entirely a précis of the notes made by my wife in Cairo, in the winter of 1928.

I have stopped short with the end of the Bronze Age, first because nothing Geometric has as yet come to light in Egypt,[1] and secondly because objects of the Orientalizing Period centre round Naucratis and have been dealt with at length in the publications of that site.

As will be seen from a glance at the accompanying map, the finds are well scattered from south of the Delta to Lower Nubia. Their absence from the Delta is due solely to the fact that expense has made excavation in that region almost impossible.

The finds from the two earliest sites are the most important from the chronological point of view. Lahun and Harageh give a definite date for Kamares ware (M.M. II), for the former at least can be accurately dated to the reign of Senusert II of the XIIth Dynasty, c. 1903–1887. The fine vase from Abydos also is well stratified in a XIIth Dynasty grave.

In discussing the later period, I would like to say that I do not employ the terms "Late Minoan" and "Late Helladic" in any controversial sense, but merely in order shortly to distinguish truly Cretan pottery from pottery which seems to show more affinities with typical examples from the Mainland and Rhodes.

Late Minoan I *a* is found at Anibe in Nubia. Late Minoan I *b* at Lahun and in a grave at Saqqara, the former in a rather doubtful context—the latter in an undoubted XVIIIth Dynasty grave. To Late Minoan I *b* also belong the fine oenochoe known as the Marseilles vase and a squat bowl said to come from Armant.[2] Late Helladic I is found at Abousir, and in the above-mentioned grave at Saqqara.

Late Minoan II is not found in Egypt,[3] unless we are to count as such the fragments from the tomb of Mentu-her-khepshef at Thebes. That vase, however, seems to be more closely connected with the pseudo-Palace style of the Mainland.

Late Minoan III does not appear at all in Egypt.[4] All the pottery that has hitherto gone under that name approximates in decoration and fabric to that of Rhodes[5] and the Mainland. This pottery first appears in the Palace of Amenhotep III and is found in quantities during the succeeding reign at Tell el Amarna. It continues down through the XIXth Dynasty, where it appears as far south as Assuan, and is found in a XXth

---

[1] The Geometric vase in the Cairo Museum, Room 39 (v), Case D, No. 26,134, is a gift and does not come from Egypt.

[2] Context quite unknown.

[3] See above, p. 4.　　　　　　　　　　　　　　　　[4] Cf. p. xviii, note 4.

[5] The importance of this early contact with Rhodes and the persistent connection between the two places I hope to show in my report to Professor Maiuri on the Egyptian finds at Ialysos.

Dynasty tomb at Mostai. Its widespread influence may be seen in the extraordinary number of imitation stirrup vases made of faience which appear during this later period. The last example, Late Helladic III, seems to be that from Der el Baḥri in the grave of a grandson of Pinezem I (XXIst Dynasty, eleventh century B.C.) though the context is appallingly corrupt.[1]

Abousir	L.H. I cup	Pits of the Dogs	*Arch. Anz.* 1899, p. 57, fig. 1. Cairo Museum, No. 26,124
Abydos	M.M. II *b* vase	XIIth Dynasty grave	*Liverpool Annals*, 1913, p. 107, Pls. 13, 14. Ashmolean Museum
	L.H. III stirrup vase	XVIIIth Dynasty house	Petrie, *Abydos III*, p. 38, Pl. 58
	L.H. III stirrup vase	Gadra	Edgar, *Catalogue of Greek Vases in the Cairo Museum*. Cairo Museum, No. 26,129
Anibe	L.M. I *a* squat bowl	Early XVIIIth Dynasty grave	*Pennsylvania Museum Journ.* I. p. 47 ff., fig. 31
Armant	L.M. I *b* squat bowl	Context unknown	Perrot, Chipiez, VI. p. 925, fig. 485. British Museum
Assiut	L.H. III stirrup vase	Context unknown	Cairo Museum, No. 46,224
Assuan	L.H. III stirrup vase	XIXth Dynasty grave Necropolis 131	Elephantine Museum
Balabish	L.H. III stirrup vases	New Kingdom cemetery	Wainwright, *Balabish*, pp. 65, 66, Pl. XXV. Cairo Museum, No. 47,084
Gurob	L.M. I *a* squat bowl L.H. III vases	XVIIIth Dynasty grave XVIIIth and XIXth Dynasty houses and graves	Petrie, *Kahun*, etc., Pl. XXVIII, Nos. 1 and 7; *Illahun*, etc., Pls. XVII, XIX, XX. Brunton and Engelbach, *Gurob*, Pls. XIII, XXIX. Loat, *Gurob*, Pl. 17, No. 5. Cairo Museum, No. 47,079. Ashmolean Museum, Brussels, etc.
Harageh	M.M. II *a* sherds	Rubbish over XIIth Dynasty shaft graves	Engelbach, *Harageh*, p. 10; *P. of M.* II. 1. fig. 119
Lahun	M.M. II sherds[2]	Workmen's village of Senusert II (XIIth Dynasty)	Petrie, *Kahun*, etc., p. 21 ff.; *Illahun*, etc., p. 5, Pl. L. British Museum
	L.M. I *b* squat bowl	Tomb of Maket, XXth Dynasty (later said to be XVIIIth)	Petrie, *Illahun*, etc., Pl. XXVI. Ashmolean Museum

[1] See Fimmen, p. 167 and note 7.
[2] The sherds called Middle Helladic in the *Catalogue of Vases in the British Museum*, Vol. I. Part I. A. 278–9, are in reality, Mr R. W. Hutchinson tells me, Syrian.

Memphis	L.H. III sherd from stirrup vase	Temple of Merenptah (XIXth Dynasty)	Petrie, *Memphis*, II. p. 15, Pl. XXII. No. 4
Mostai	L.H. III stirrup vase	XXth Dynasty Necropolis	*Annales du Service des Antiquités*, XII. pp. 209–213. Cairo Museum, No. 43,735
Naqada	L.H. III stirrup vase	XVIIIth Dynasty rock tomb	Petrie and Quibell, *Naqada and Ballas*, p. 69
Rifeh	L.H. III vases	XVIIIth and XIXth Dynasty graves	Petrie, *Gizeh and Rifeh*, Pls. XXIII and XXVII
Riqqeh	L.H. III stirrup vases	XVIIIth and XIXth Dynasty graves	Engelbach, *Riqqeh*, Pl. XXII
Saqqara	L.M. I *b* squat bowl; L.H. I saucer	XVIIIth Dynasty grave	Firth and Gunn, *Saqqara*, Pl. XLII. Cairo Museum, Nos. 47,772, 47,773
	L.H. III vase	Old Kingdom grave	Lepsius, *Denkmäler Text*, I. No. 1244. Furtwängler, *Mykenische Vasen*, p. 31, No. 159
Sedment	L.H. III stirrup vases	XVIIIth and XIXth Dynasty graves	Petrie and Brunton, *Sedment*, Pls. LIX, LXV. Cairo Museum, No. 47,011. Ashmolean Museum
Tell el Amarna	L.H. III sherds	Palace rubbish heap and houses of XVIIIth Dynasty	Forsdyke, *Catalogue of Vases in the British Museum*, Vol. I. Part I. p. 183 ff. and references on p. 184
Thebes	L.H. II? vase	Tomb of Mentu-her-khepshef (XIXth Dynasty)	Davis, *Five Theban Tombs*, Pl. XLI. Ashmolean Museum
	L.H. III stirrup vases	Gurna	Edgar, *Catalogue of Greek Vases in the Cairo Museum*, p. 3. Cairo Museum, No. 26,131
	L.H. III cup and sherds	Palace of Amenhotep III (XVIIIth Dynasty)	*Arch. Anz.* 1899, p. 57
	L.H. III stirrup vase	Grave of grandson of Pinezem I (XXIst Dynasty)	Hall, *Oldest Civilization of Greece*, p. 62, fig. 28. British Museum, No. 22,821
Also *Unknown Provenance*	L.M. I *a* squat bowls		Cairo Museum, Nos. 26,125, 26,126
	L.M. I *b* oenochoe		Marseilles Museum, No. 1043
	L.H. III stirrup vases		Cairo Museum, Nos. 26,127, 26,128, 26,130, 26,132, 26,133

TABLE OF OBJECTS ACCORDING TO
POTTERY STRATA

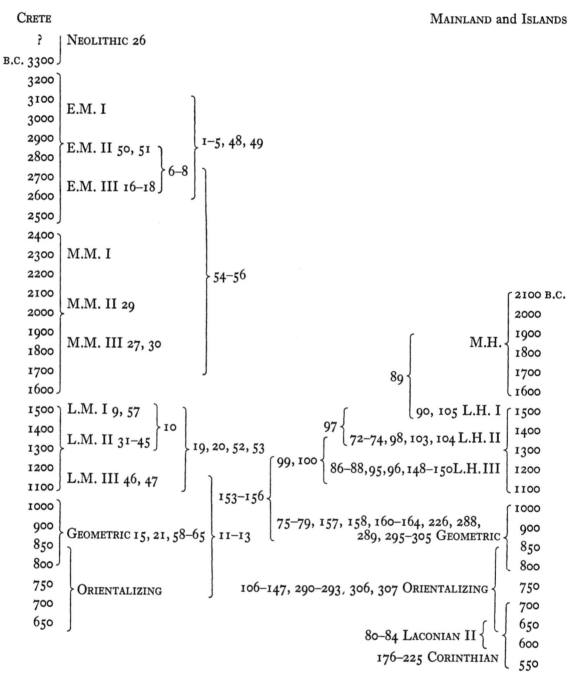

CRETE   MAINLAND and ISLANDS

Crete		Mainland and Islands

? | NEOLITHIC 26

B.C. 3300

3200

3100   E.M. I

3000

2900   E.M. II 50, 51   } 1–5, 48, 49

2800

2700   E.M. III 16–18   } 6–8

2600

2500

2400

2300   M.M. I

2200

2100   } 54–56

2000   M.M. II 29

1900   M.M. III 27, 30   2100 B.C.
                                                                      2000
1800   M.H. { 1900
1700   89 {   1800
1600   1700
                                                                      1600

1500   L.M. I 9, 57   }   90, 105 L.H. I { 1500
1400   L.M. II 31–45 } 10   } 19, 20, 52, 53   97 {   1400
1300   72–74, 98, 103, 104 L.H. II 1300
1200   L.M. III 46, 47   } 99, 100 { 86–88, 95, 96, 148–150 L.H. III 1200
1100   1100

1000   153–156 {   1000
900   GEOMETRIC 15, 21, 58–65 } 11–13   75–79, 157, 158, 160–164, 226, 288,   900
850   289, 295–305 GEOMETRIC { 850
800   800

750   ORIENTALIZING   106–147, 290–293, 306, 307 ORIENTALIZING { 750
700   700
650   650
                                          80–84 LACONIAN II {   600
                                       176–225 CORINTHIAN   550

UNSTRATIFIED   14, 22–25, 28, 66–71, 85, 91–94, 101, 102, 151, 152, 159, 165–   UNSTRATIFIED
                                    175, 227–287, 294

TABLE OF OBJECTS ACCORDING TO DYNASTIES

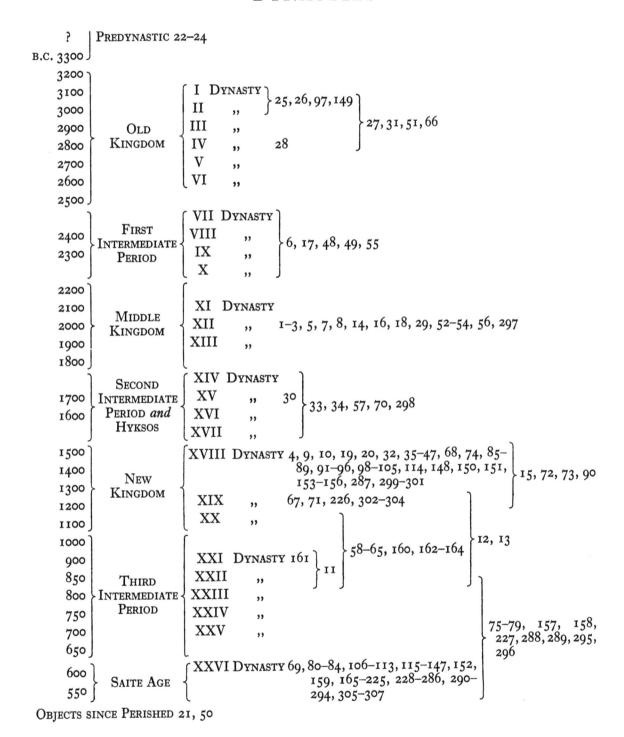

?   PREDYNASTIC 22–24

B.C. 3300

3200
3100   I DYNASTY   } 25, 26, 97, 149
3000   II   „
2900   OLD   III   „   } 27, 31, 51, 66
2800   KINGDOM   IV   „   28
2700   V   „
2600   VI   „
2500

2400   FIRST   VII DYNASTY
       INTERMEDIATE   VIII   „   } 6, 17, 48, 49, 55
2300   PERIOD   IX   „
       X   „

2200
2100   XI DYNASTY
2000   MIDDLE   XII   „   1–3, 5, 7, 8, 14, 16, 18, 29, 52–54, 56, 297
1900   KINGDOM   XIII   „
1800

1700   SECOND   XIV DYNASTY
       INTERMEDIATE   XV   „   30   } 33, 34, 57, 70, 298
1600   PERIOD and   XVI   „
       HYKSOS   XVII   „

1500   XVIII DYNASTY 4, 9, 10, 19, 20, 32, 35–47, 68, 74, 85–
1400   NEW   89, 91–96, 98–105, 114, 148, 150, 151,   } 15, 72, 73, 90
1300   KINGDOM   153–156, 287, 299–301
1200   XIX   „   67, 71, 226, 302–304
1100   XX   „

1000
900   XXI DYNASTY 161 }   } 58–65, 160, 162–164   } 12, 13
850   THIRD   XXII   „   } 11
800   INTERMEDIATE   XXIII   „
750   PERIOD   XXIV   „
700   XXV   „   } 75–79, 157, 158,
650   227, 288, 289, 295, 296

600   SAITE AGE   XXVI DYNASTY 69, 80–84, 106–113, 115–147, 152,
550   159, 165–225, 228–286, 290–
294, 305–307

OBJECTS SINCE PERISHED 21, 50

115

LIST OF MUSEUMS IN WHICH THE OBJECTS
ARE TO BE FOUND

TYPES OF OBJECTS AND THEIR MATERIALS

AMULETS:
CRYSTAL, 135
FAIENCE, 43, 134, 136–141, 184, 185, 187, 189–191, 236–238, 240–242, 253, 255, 263, 267–271, 274, 291–293
LAPIS LAZULI, 8, 44, 45
PASTE, 261

BEADS:
AMETHYST AND CARNELIAN, 57
CARNELIAN, STEATITE AND FAIENCE, 65
FAIENCE, 16, 51
LAPIS LAZULI, 42

FIGURINES:
FAIENCE, 85, 146, 147, 157, 158, 160, 183, 186, 188, 249–252, 288, 306
PASTE, 77, 262

INDETERMINATE FRAGMENTS OF FAIENCE, 21, 86, 87, 142, 175, 272

MACE HEAD:
DIORITE, 24

SCARABS:
AMETHYST, 1, 14
FAIENCE, 67, 69, 84, 106–112, 114, 116–125, 128–133, 161–174, 200–207, 221, 225, 254, 276–283, 289, 297–305; on BRONZE RING, 275; on SILVER RING, 295
ONYX, 5
PASTE, 4, 6, 12, 13, 68, 75, 76, 80–83, 88, 95, 96, 105, 115, 176–181, 199, 208–220, 222, 228–235, 256, 257, 296
POTTERY, 126, 127
STEATITE, 2, 3, 17, 18, 47, 49, 54–56, 70, 71, 113, 226

SCARABOID:
CARNELIAN, 151

SEALS:
FAIENCE, 58–64
PASTE, 7, 182, 192–198, 223, 224
STEATITE, 10, 48

SPINDLE WHORLS:
FAIENCE, 78, 79, 144, 145, 244–248, 258–260, 264, 284–286, 290

SPOONS:
? IVORY, 150
SILVER, 73

STATUETTES:
BRONZE, 15, 159, 294
DIORITE, 29
IVORY, 52, 53

(USHABTI:
FAIENCE, unnumbered, from Mistra)

VASES:
BRONZE, 227
CLAY, 92–94, 152–156
FAIENCE, 11, 50, 89–91, 103, 143, 243, 265, 266, 273, 307
STONE:
ALABASTER, 9, 19, 20, 30, 32–41, 46, 72, 74, 98–102, 104, 148, 239, 287
DIORITE, 27, 28, 31, 66
HORNBLENDE PORPHYRY, 22, 23, 25, 97, 149
SYENITE, 26

OBJECTS BEARING THE NAMES OF
KINGS OR QUEENS

Se-user-en-Ra (Khyan)	18th century B.C. (?)	XVth Dynasty	No. 30 (lid of alabastron)
Men-kheper-Ra (Thothmes III)	1501–1447 B.C.	XVIIIth Dynasty	No. 114 (scarab)
Aa-kheperu-Ra (Amenhotep II)	1447–1420 B.C.	XVIIIth Dynasty	No. 85 (faience ape)
Neb-Maat-Ra (Amenhotep III)	1412–1376 B.C.	XVIIIth Dynasty	No. 86 (faience plaque) No. 91 (faience vase)
Royal Wife Tiyi (Queen of Amenhotep III)		XVIIIth Dynasty	No. 10 (seal) No. 88 (scarab)
Men-kheper-Ra	c. 1050 B.C.	XXIst Dynasty	No. 161 (scarab)
Uah-ab-Ra (Psamtek I)	663–609 B.C.	XXVIth Dynasty	No. 152 (clay vase)

GENERAL INDEX TO THE TEXT APART FROM THE CATALOGUE PROPER

The heavy type gives the reference to the complete sections dealing with the place mentioned

PLATE I

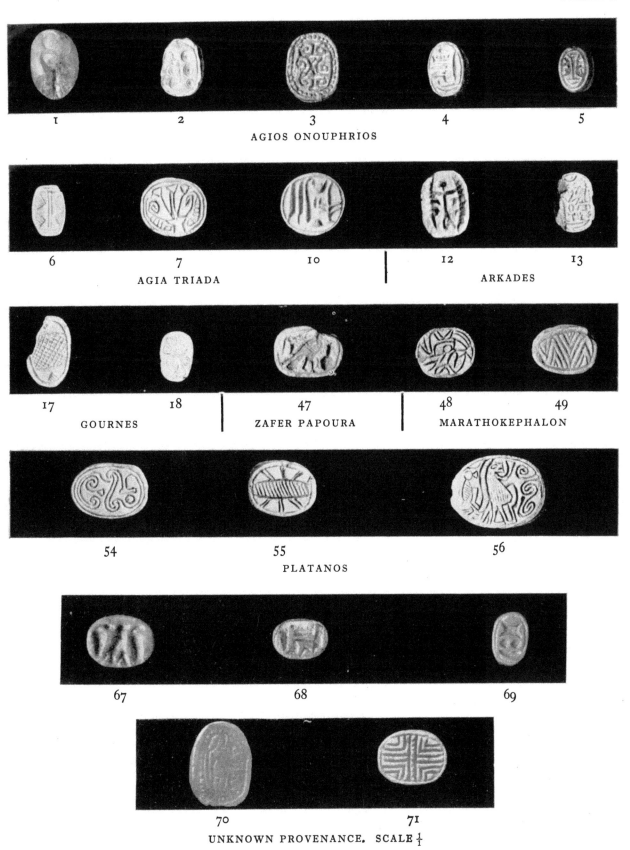

1   2   3   4   5
AGIOS ONOUPHRIOS

6   7   10   12   13
AGIA TRIADA   ARKADES

17   18   47   48   49
GOURNES   ZAFER PAPOURA   MARATHOKEPHALON

54   55   56
PLATANOS

67   68   69

70   71
UNKNOWN PROVENANCE. SCALE ¼

PLATE II

25. SCALE $\frac{3}{7}$

26. SCALE $\frac{2}{5}$

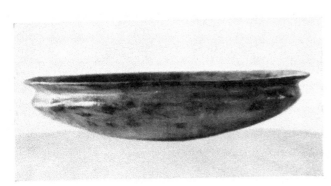

27. SCALE $\frac{2}{5}$

28. SCALE $\frac{1}{6}$

29. SCALE $\frac{1}{2}$

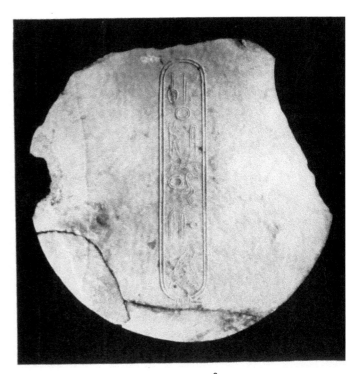

30. SCALE $\frac{3}{4}$

KNOSSOS

PLATE III

226

THEBES. SCALE ¼

52   53

PALAIKASTRO. SCALE ½

227

VELESTINO. SCALE ½

35   36   37   39

ISOPATA. SCALE ⅔

PLATE IV

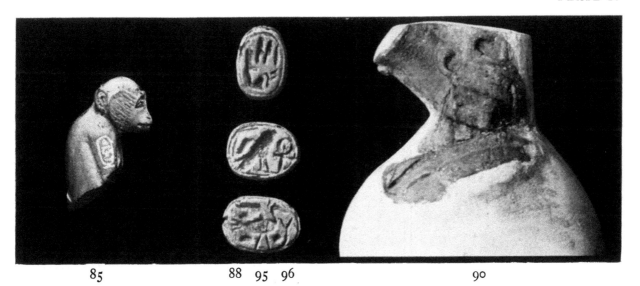

85   88 95 96   90

MYCENAE. SCALE $\frac{1}{1}$

159

ATHENS. SCALE $\frac{1}{1}$

178   179   181
182   205   213
219   220   183
184   185

SUNIUM. SCALE $\frac{1}{1}$

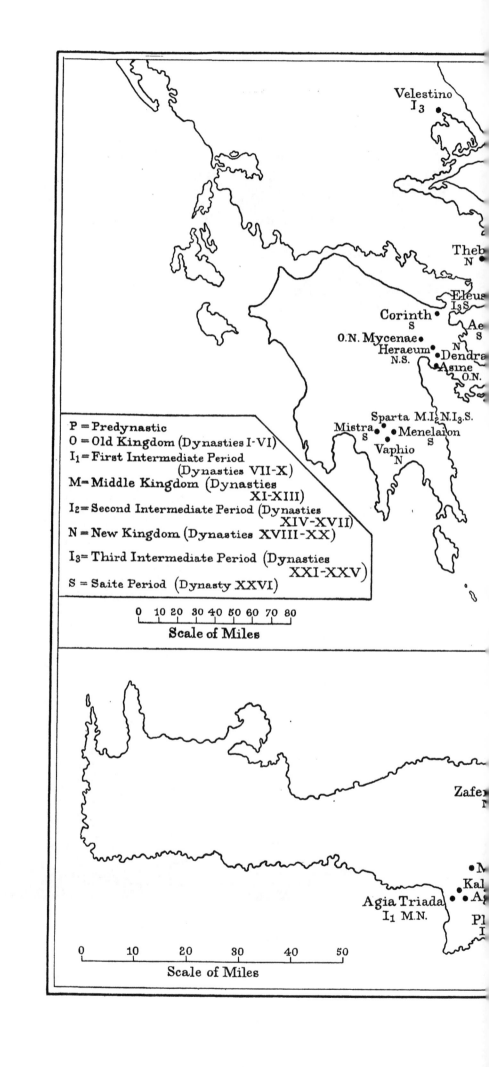

Velestino
I₃

Theb
N

Eleus
I₃S

Corinth
S

Ae
S

O.N. Mycenae
N
Heraeum   Dendra
N.S.   Asine
O.N.

Sparta M.I₂N.I₃.S.
Mistra   Menelaion
S   S
Vaphio
N

P = Predynastic
O = Old Kingdom (Dynasties I-VI)
I₁ = First Intermediate Period
          (Dynasties VII-X)
M = Middle Kingdom (Dynasties
                    XI-XIII)
I₂ = Second Intermediate Period (Dynasties
                                 XIV-XVII)
N = New Kingdom (Dynasties XVIII-XX)
I₃ = Third Intermediate Period (Dynasties
                                XXI-XXV)
S = Saite Period (Dynasty XXVI)

0   10 20 30 40 50 60 70 80
Scale of Miles

Zafe
N

M
Kal
Agia Triada   A
I₁ M.N.
              Pl
              I

0   10   20   30   40   50
Scale of Miles

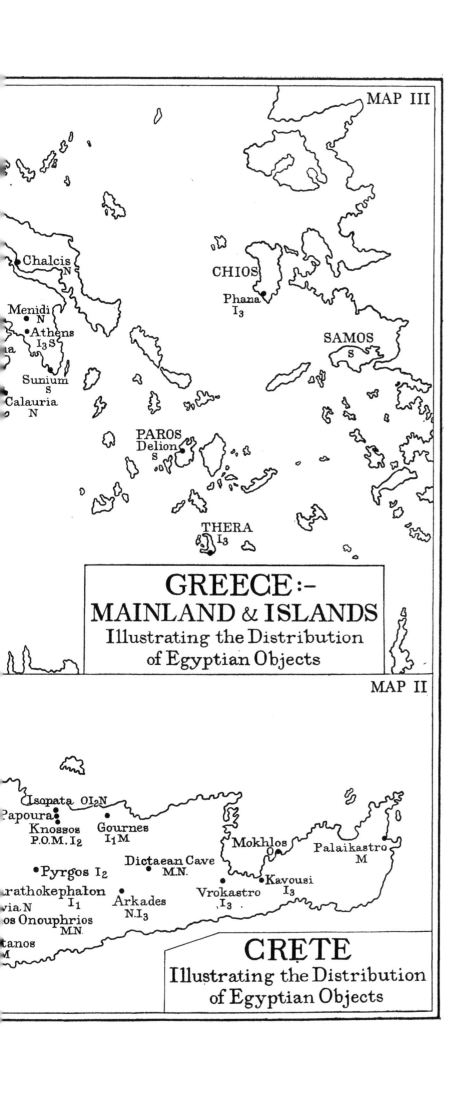

MAP III

Chalcis
N

Menidi
N
Athens
I₃ S

Sunium
S

Calauria
N

CHIOS

Phana
I₃

SAMOS
S

PAROS
Delion
S

THERA I₃

GREECE :-
MAINLAND & ISLANDS
Illustrating the Distribution
of Egyptian Objects

MAP II

Isopata OI₂N

Papoura

Knossos
P.O.M. I₂

Gournes
I₁ M

Mokhlos
O

Palaikastro
M

Pyrgos I₂

Dictaean Cave
M.N.

Kavousi
I₃

rathokephalon
I₁

via N

os Onouphrios
M.N.

Arkades
N.I₃

Vrokastro
I₃

tanos
M

CRETE
Illustrating the Distribution
of Egyptian Objects

For EU product safety concerns, contact us at Calle de José Abascal, 56–1°,
28003 Madrid, Spain or eugpsr@cambridge.org.

www.ingramcontent.com/pod-product-compliance
Ingram Content Group UK Ltd.
Pitfield, Milton Keynes, MK11 3LW, UK
UKHW050455190625
459647UK00035B/2864